PRAISE FOR

Lowestoft Chronicle

I0653246

"My two major complaints about numerous online literary magazines are they are so confusing and disorganized [and] stories are boring and the poetry is derivative and lacking in creativity. I am happy to say that this young journal manages to avoid these pitfalls. *Lowestoft Chronicle* is nicely laid out and presents entertaining and exciting stories that lend themselves toward travel without dipping completely over into travel writing." —Newpages.com

"Travel writers, here's a great place for your work. A tip of the hat (sombrero, fez) to *Lowestoft Chronicle* for fueling our urge to turn off *Jersey Shore*, toss our cell phones into a lake, and go embrace this amazing planet of ours. Bon Voyage!"

—Franz Wisner, *New York Times* bestselling author of *Honeymoon with My brother*

"Go ahead, read it right now. I'll wait... Fun, huh? Thought it might pep up your midweek. All things considered, it might just be a very good thing if the *Lowestoft Chronicle* were to achieve their goal of world domination. Best wishes to them!"
—Cheryl LaGuardia, *Library Journal*

"Something to check out when you just want to read. I used to read a lot of literary magazines. Wonderful little collections of short stories and essays that you could only find in bookstores that felt like home. It wasn't until I ran across lowestoftchronicle.com that I realized just how long it has been. The *Lowestoft Chronicle* gets around both problems... they even have a print version. It's worth a look for fans of short stories, creative non-fiction and poetry." —Dave Dempsey, Radio FM4

"*Lowestoft Chronicle* is a standout among a growing universe of online journals. Every issue delivers a cornucopia of entertaining and thought-provoking stories and articles."

—Michael C. Keith, author of the acclaimed memoir
The Next Better Place: A Father and Son on the Road

"*Lowestoft Chronicle* is a wonderful new addition to the world of creative writing." —Tony Perrottet, acclaimed travel writer and author of
The Naked Olympics

"This is a fine anthology that I found both provocative and enjoyable. Highest praise: it made me want to write short stories again."

—Luke Rhinehart, international bestselling author of
Matari, Long Voyage Back, and *The Dice Man*

"Full of great talent and exceptionally written pieces."

—*The Review Review*

"The *Lowestoft Chronicle* is both classy and fun to read. A work accomplished by careful attention to detail and quality."

— Sheldon Russell, acclaimed author of
the Hook Runyon mystery series

"Terrific anthology. The writing here is fresh, surprising, and alive. Not to be missed is the bittersweet interview with the author Augustine Funnell. (Please write more!) The book looks and feels great. If you aren't familiar with *Lowestoft Chronicle*, head on over there. They publish, on a consistent basis, excellent fiction, poetry, and non-fiction." —Nicholas Rombes, author of
A Cultural Dictionary of Punk: 1974-1982

"In its quarterly editions, this lively, creative and often provocative magazine publishes an eclectic collection of flash fiction, short stories, poetry and creative non-fiction with the emphasis firmly on humour and travel." —Pam Norfolk, *Lancashire Evening Post*

"The world may be shrinking, but it's sure not growing any less strange. That's what we learn from *Lowestoft Chronicle*—the literary equivalent of Rick's Café in *Casablanca*, where travelers of all stripes pull up a stool and swap stories at the bar. Handsomely designed and expertly curated, *Lowestoft Chronicle* drives us into the arms of experience."   —Scott Dominic Carpenter, acclaimed author of
Theory of Remainders

"I'm always impressed with the quarterly online literary magazine, *Lowestoft Chronicle*—it's filled with intriguing fiction, non-fiction, poetry, and interviews. Click on over for good reading."
—Matthew P. Mayo, Spur Award-winning author of
Tucker's Reckoning

"Reading *Lowestoft Chronicle* is like jostling through a sprawling bazaar in Tashkent or Ulaanbaatar, with eyes wide open and wits on high alert. Invigorating, too."   — Victor Robert Lee, author of
Performance Anomalies

"I was extremely impressed with the variety and quality of the writing. There's something here for everyone... A solid collection of funny and fine travel-themed stories, poetry, essays and interviews that easily fits in a back pocket or carry-on bag."
— Frank Mundo, *LA Books Examiner*

"*Lowestoft Chronicle* is a superb lit mag. It offers the kind of perceptive, humorous writing that we like here at TCR."   —*The Committee Room*

"Loosely themed around travel and adventure, this is the only literary magazine I read these days, and it's always enjoyable. A fine blend of short stories, poetry, and essays. It takes the reader to a wide variety of literary destinations, and makes even a confirmed hermit like me want to get up and go somewhere. Highly recommended."
—James Reasoner, acclaimed author of the cult classics
Texas Wind and *Dust Devils*

Books in the Lowestoft Chronicle Anthology Series

LOWESTOFT CHRONICLE 2011 ANTHOLOGY
FAR-FLUNG AND FOREIGN
INTREPID TRAVELERS
SOMEWHERE, SOMETIME...
OTHER PLACES

OTHER PLACES

EDITED BY NICHOLAS LITCHFIELD

Lowestoft
Chronicle
Press

OTHER PLACES

SUBMISSIONS

The editors welcome submissions of poetry and prose. For submission information please visit our website at www.lowestoftchronicle.com or email: submissions@lowestoftchronicle.com

Copyright © 2015 Lowestoft Chronicle Press

Introduction © 2015 Nicholas Litchfield

Additional copyright information can be found on pages 209-211.

All rights reserved. No part of this book may be used or reproduced in any manner whatsoever without written permission from the publisher except in the case of brief quotations embodied in critical articles and reviews. For information, contact
editor@lowestoftchronicle.com

Published by Lowestoft Chronicle Press, Cambridge, Massachusetts
www.lowestoftchronicle.com

First edition: July 2015

Cover design by Tara Litchfield

ISBN 13: 978-0-9825365-6-8
ISBN 10: 0-9825365-6-9

Library of Congress Control Number: 2015939134

Printed in the United States of America

CONTENTS

Introduction by Nicholas Litchfield   9

FICTION

Break and Enter, by Peter Biello   15
Shutterbugs, by David Hagerty   29
A Question Of The Tide, by Victor Robert Lee   48
The Cambodian Void: An Apology, by Soren A. Gauger   56
Mobile Homeless, by James Stark   76
Curious in Corsica: A Tale of Two Couples, by Mary Donaldson-Evans   83
Somewhere in the Heart of Rome, by Robert Sachs   92
Cathy Has Visitors, by William Quincy Belle   109
Uprisings at Cap d'Antibes, by Robert Mangeot   117
The Sibyl, by John Mueter   141
Antique Roses, by Robert Boucheron   150
Survival of the Fittest, by Allister Timms   158
The Hill Behind the House, by Michael C. Keith   167
Segway with the Bulls, by Geoffrey B. Cain   174
The High Colonic, by Raymond Abbott   179

POETRY

Bangkok of the Mind, by Stephen Cloud   55
To The Passenger In Seat C, by dl mattila   82
Shooing Flies, by David Havird   101
Midrash, by Jay Parini   140
Enter the Travellers, by Joe Mills   173

CREATIVE NON-FICTION

Via Dolorosa, by Matt Nestor   23

My Driver, Sunday, by Mona Zutshi Opubor   67

A Farewell to Farms, by Kevin Quigley   103

Rescue in the Mystical Mountains, by C.B. Heinemann   128

Danish as She is Spoke, by Scott Dominic Carpenter   191

INTERVIEW

A Conversation with Sheldon Russell | 39

A Conversation with Jay Parini | 133

A Conversation with Scott Dominic Carpenter | 183

CONTRIBUTORS | 202
COPYRIGHT NOTES | 209
ACKNOWLEDGEMENTS | 212

INTRODUCTION

Nicholas Litchfield

Author Scott Dominic Carpenter once described *Lowestoft Chronicle* as "the literary equivalent of Rick's Café in *Casablanca*, where travelers of all stripes pull up a stool and swap stories at the bar." Founded in 2009 and published quarterly, *Lowestoft Chronicle* is an online journal of new writing, loosely themed around travel. The name of the magazine was inspired by the English coastal town of Lowestoft, in Suffolk, which was, a long time ago, a regular weekend getaway destination of mine. While, I admit, it might not be considered the prettiest of coastal towns, there is, nevertheless, a tranquil charm about the place that led me to keep returning. For some reason, there's always been a scarcity of periodicals produced there. Four or five newspapers existed at one time, but now only the weekly tabloid *Lowestoft Journal* remains. I wanted to give something back to the town, and I felt it could certainly do with another publication, and so, I named a magazine in its honor—one with a literary feel and an emphasis on travel. I am proud to say that *Lowestoft Chronicle* carries the distinction of being the town's first and only literary magazine.

Each year, we produce a print anthology of the best pieces from the online editions of the magazine. The first one, published in 2011, was about the thickness of two beer coasters pressed together, though far more durable. Since then, the books have become progressively fatter. I like to think that this latest one is perhaps the perfect breadth and size to serve a round of cocktails on, thus making it multi-purpose.

As with previous books, this one is chock-full of short yet satisfying moments of high drama. Among the more exotic adventures here—in Cambodia, bloody havoc ensues when a puddle of brown sauce on a restaurant table wrecks a routine business meeting in "The Cambodian Void: An Apology," by Soren A. Gauger. In Brazil, an attractive, flirtatious woman leads a surfer to battle more than just the waves in Victor Robert Lee's "A Question Of The Tide." In Robert Mangeot's "Uprisings at Cap d'Antibes," a revolution begins at a tennis academy on the French Riviera. And in Geoffrey B. Cain's "Segway with the Bulls," disaster strikes at the festival of San Fermin in Pamplona, Spain, when the Running of the Bulls event takes a dangerous turn.

There's also a generous assortment of humorous prose, such as "Survival of the Fittest," by Allister Timms, where a boy's elocution lesson goes madly awry when a parrot decides to get fully involved. In William Quincy Belle's darkly comic "Cathy Has Visitors," burglars come face to face with a strong-willed, dangerous seventy-eight year old woman. And in "The Sibyl," by John Mueter, a university scholar discovers an extraordinary book in a public library that leads him on an adventure through Greece to converse with the prophetess Sibyl.

Other delightfully amusing tales include Peter Biello's "Break and Enter," where a young man turns to housebreaking in an ill-fated attempt to repair his relationship with a former sweetheart. In Mary Donaldson-Evans' "Curious in Corsica: A Tale of Two Couples," a married couple's tiff in the dining room of a Corsican hotel spurs an eavesdropper to investigate the unhappy couple's relationship with startling results. In "Somewhere in the Heart of Rome," by Robert Sachs, a lonely vacationer taking in the tourist hotspots of Rome finds himself photographing a beautiful, topless woman—at her request. And in "The High Colonic," Raymond Abbott drolly recalls an ill-conceived attempt to "say the right thing" after a table companion has confided a personal tragedy.

Elsewhere, a collector of old roses discovers a specimen in

Virginia that holds particularly significant roots, in "Antique Roses" by Robert Boucheron. During the course of a rescue, a park ranger investigates an injured hiker's claim that he was bushwhacked, in "Shutterbugs," by David Hagerty. And in James Stark's "Mobile Homeless," community concern grows over a rusty Volkswagen van that remains parked in front of a man's house in a quiet suburban neighborhood in Seattle.

If *Lowestoft Chronicle* can be compared to Rick's Café in *Casablanca*, then prolific science-fiction writer Michael C. Keith might well be considered "a regular." To date, his thrilling stories have appeared in ten issues of the magazine. Included here is his spooky tale "The Hill Behind the House," concerning the fate of a twelve-year-old boy who's fearlessly determined to discover what lurks beyond the hill at the back of his family's ranch—whatever the cost.

All too often, the nonfiction pieces we receive seem so fantastic that we mistake them for fiction. Some of the best out-of-the-ordinary pieces from last year include "My Driver, Sunday," by Mona Zutshi Opubor, a humorous account of woman's adjustment to life in Lagos, Nigeria, through her evolving relationship with her hazardous driver; Matt Nestor's "Via Dolorosa," where he recounts his daring couch-surfing experiences across the U.S.; "A Farewell to Farms," by Kevin Quigley, where a young man staying in a farmhouse in France learning homesteading skills is unnerved by his reclusive host; and C.B. Heinemann's "Rescue in the Mystical Mountains," where stray dogs lead a couple on an illuminating adventure through the Montserrat mountain range in Spain.

As with previous anthologies, this one contains a varied assortment of succinct and exquisitely crafted poems. In "Bangkok of the Mind," Stephen Cloud stimulates the senses as he steadfastly explores the overwhelming, labyrinthine city of Bangkok. Jay Parini enlivens the spirit through his lucid reflections about God in the religious poem "Midrash." In the whimsical "To The Passenger In Seat C," poet dl mattila wittily bemoans her fellow passenger for blessing her soul every time she sneezes. Smart use of imagery and adroit humor heighten an affectionate rendezvous at a ferry port, in "Shooing Flies" by David Havird. And in "Enter the Travellers," Joe Mills utilizes Shakespeare's stage directions to craft an intriguing poem pondering the Bard's "lost" years.

Over the years, I've been very privileged to be able to interview some of my absolute favorite authors. Sometimes, the conversations blossom into full-length interviews and are published in the magazine, and sometimes they don't seem quite substantial enough for inclusion. For this anthology, I'm very proud to include my in-depth conversations with three highly acclaimed and especially versatile authors. The first is with Sheldon Russell, an award-winning author of historical fiction and a Spur-award finalist. Despite his enormous success writing about the McReynolds kinfolk, he is perhaps best known for his Hook Runyon mystery series, which has received great reviews in the *New York Times* and starred reviews from *Booklist* and *Publishers Weekly*. In this interview, he discusses his historical novels, his distinctive one-armed railroad detective Hook Runyon, and some of his work in progress.

The second interview is with poet, novelist, and biographer Jay Parini, editor of countless volumes of anthologies and literary criticism and author of dozens of books, from bestselling novels like *The Last Station*, and widely praised poetry collections like *Anthracite Country*, to critically-acclaimed biographies of John Steinbeck, Robert Frost, William Faulkner, and Jesus. Back in 2010, I was very fortunate to be able to see him in person— he hosted a discussion on the evolution of the novel at the Boston Book Festival. For me, the highlight of the discussion, and indeed the festival, was listening to Jay discuss some of the great writers he's met, his experiences living abroad, and anecdotes about people like Gore Vidal and Anthony Quinn.

In his interview with *Lowestoft Chronicle*, he discusses his poetry, his most recent biography, and the early days of his writing career studying overseas in Scotland.

The last of the interviews is with Scott Dominic Carpenter, a professor of French literature and literary theory, whose highly acclaimed debut novel, *Theory of Remainders*, is one of the most suspenseful books I've read in years. My interview with him explores that book, as well as his debut story collection, *This Jealous Earth*. This anthology also contains his nonfiction piece "Danish as She is Spoke," an amusing account of his experiences in Denmark and his attempts to master the language.

So, grab yourself that Scotch and soda, pull up a stool, and drink in our latest collection of travel-inspired poetry and prose.

BREAK AND ENTER

Peter Biello

Technically it wasn't a break-in because I still had the key she gave me. There was no breaking involved, and since she never took the key back or changed the lock, there was an implicit invitation to enter anytime I wanted. It's true we hadn't spoken in months, but in my defense, I had no intention of going inside without her. I thought, if she's home, she'll either slam the door on my face or invite me in to talk about what happened. If she's not home, I'll just leave the blueberry pie and the note on her doormat and call it a night.

So with a pounding heart and a pie in my hands, I stood at the end of a narrow hallway, staring at the brass knocker on her door. Her name is Eliza. Among the many things I learned about Eliza, in the two months we dated, was her love of blueberry pie. She also loved Ray LaMontagne, Cuba, salsa dancing, yoga, meditation, architecture, and her daily Zumba class. The pie was meant to show her that I had been listening to her, that I still cared for her (to borrow LaMontagne's lyric), and that I wanted a second chance. I knocked.

Nothing. Now I suppose on some level I knew she wouldn't be home. It was Thursday, and every Thursday after Zumba she went to her parents' place for dinner. At that moment she was probably chatting with them about architecture (both were architects) and dining on some healthy post-workout meal like arugula and pear salad with walnuts and a light balsamic. Perhaps if I hadn't cut off our relationship, I'd be there with her right now. But then again, it had been more than three months since I'd last seen her. Routines change.

I knocked again. No answer.

I discovered that I was relieved she wasn't home. There would be no angry slamming of doors, no brutal rejection. I began to put the pie on the ground when, suddenly, a flash of yellow fur descended on the box. A dog. I pulled the box out of its reach. A golden lab sat at my feet, its eyes on the pie, nose twitching.

"Rocky, come here!" an elderly woman across the hall called. A memory returned: Eliza and I wrapping up our third date, our bodies buzzing with wine, and this neighbor was letting Rocky out. I remembered this old woman's glasses and how they magnified her eyes. "I'm sorry," she said, searching my face with those big eyes. "Did he scratch you?"

"No, no, I'm fine," I said. My heart pounded. I felt like she'd caught me in the act of something sinister.

"He won't bite," she said. "Though he may eat your pie if you're not careful. I usually leave him out in the hallway while I vacuum."

"No problem. How long does it take to vacuum?"

"About fifteen minutes," she said. "Maybe twenty. Rocky sheds like you wouldn't believe. And he *hates* the vacuum."

I realized then that I didn't want to come back in fifteen minutes, because Eliza might be home then, and I was too afraid to confront her. And that's when I remembered the key. My fingers reached into my pocket and fingered its sharp notches. As if I'd done it a thousand times, I pulled out the key and put it into her lock. "Have a good night," I said, and went inside.

"Tell Eliza I said hi," I heard her say as I closed the door behind me.

It was a mistake. I felt that in my core. I stood there in Eliza's kitchen, looking around, too afraid to move. The apartment hadn't changed since the night I broke things off. That night, we sat on her sofa and I told her I wasn't ready to be in a relationship, which was only partly true. The rest of the truth was: I knew I was falling in love with her, and I was certain a smart, kind, beautiful woman like her would break my heart. "Well, we can just be friends and take things slow," she said, her green eyes searching me for the reason behind my actions. "We have a real connection. Why would you do this?" At the time, I told myself she wasn't really sad, just disappointed that I wouldn't keep her company until someone better came along. "I just can't," I'd said. "I'm sorry." I hugged her and left. I didn't even cry. I felt like I'd done a good job of protecting myself. The tears came later, in my therapist's office, when I realized I was wrong.

So there I was, standing in her kitchen with a blueberry pie. Across the hall, the neighbor's vacuum hummed. Given the circumstances, I should have left the key and the pie on the kitchen table and walked out. Had I left then, I could have explained to her later that I didn't mean to enter her place, but the dog would've eaten her pie. But I didn't. Instead, I put the pie on the kitchen table, opened the door and depressed the lock button on the knob, and began my exit, but right before I closed the door, I stopped. If she was following her workout routine—and she probably was—I had at least an hour until she made it home. I was already there. And her stuff—not the buried stuff, but the stuff just laying around—could tell me something about her life. So why not take a quick look around? Just a glance, nothing more. Sixty seconds, tops.

I let the door close and lock me inside. Passing through the kitchen to the living room, I noticed, on the coffee table, an anthology of Latin American poetry. On our first date at this apartment, we sat on that sofa and she read aloud to me. I don't speak Spanish, but I wanted to see if I could glean the emotional content, maybe catch a glimpse of the beauty she saw. I couldn't. But she told me it was about stars, and there were other meanings that would be lost in translation, and wouldn't it be lovely if we could travel to Cuba together?

"That would be great," I'd said, thinking: She's going to leave me for some handsome Cuban. Now, before you think I'm being unreasonable, consider two things she said that made her breaking up with me seem inevitable. One: "I've been the one to end every relationship I've been in." Two: "You're the first white guy I've dated since college." If that's the case, then maybe she doesn't really like white guys, and if *that's* the case, what is she doing with an Irish-American ginger like me? The whole thing made no sense. Even as she had heaped praise on me—about how she found me handsome, hard-working, and kind—I couldn't see why she wanted me.

I entered her bedroom. Her pillows were scattered on the hardwood floor and her blanket hung crookedly over the mattress. Beside her bed was her diary. I knew it would be; I'd seen it there the night we lay in bed, curled up together, fully clothed, talking and kissing until I had to catch the bus home. I stood there, looking at her diary, a little book with "I avoid clichés like the plague" on the cover, and I hoped that something else about the room would tell me about what her life was like now, because I didn't want to open it. It felt wrong, whereas everything until that moment—yes, even walking around her apartment—felt like an accident.

I was walking back into the living room when the vacuum stopped and I heard the sound of a key in the door. I froze. For a moment, I simply couldn't believe it. But I knew the sound of her keys. Eliza was home.

I thought I should shout hello, so she wouldn't be frightened at the sight of a man in her apartment. But for some reason, I decided not to—though to say I was making any "decisions" in those panicked moments would be a stretch—and as the door swung open, I backpedaled into her bedroom, dropped to my belly, shimmied under her bed and covered my hiding spot with the blanket.

As soon as I did it, I wished I hadn't. My heart was pounding so loudly I was sure she could hear it. I breathed deeply, inhaled dust, and then stifled a cough. She dropped her keys on the table, next to the pie. Then I heard the soft shuffle of cardboard as she opened the box.

There was a long pause. And then my cell phone vibrated.

"You came into my apartment," Eliza's text message read. She was not angry, not yet. She was putting the fact between us to see how I'd handle it.

"I'm sorry," I wrote back. "I wanted to leave the pie on the doorstep, but there was a dog in the hallway."

"I must have just missed you. The dog is still out there," she texted. Her footsteps grew louder until they stopped next to the bed. I imagined her looking around the room, scanning for moved or missing items. I was thinking of a reply when I heard her say aloud: "Hey, you're not going to believe this. Mike came into my apartment when I was out and left a pie in my kitchen."

The lamp on the nightstand clicked on. The bed creaked under her weight. "Yeah, I know," she said. "Yeah, totally. I'm a little freaked out. Not a word for three months and then, surprise! Here's a pie."

My heart began to pound. I began imagining alternate universes in which I was not hiding under her bed. In one, I shortened my shower by a few minutes, dressed myself a bit faster, and took an earlier bus. In another, I took a later bus and arrived after she returned home. Shoulda coulda woulda, said the man under the bed.

"Well, I gave him a key, but I never asked for it back," she told someone, probably her best friend, Janie. "He just sent me a text saying that he was going to leave the pie on the floor in the hallway, but there was a dog outside, and the dog would have eaten it. So I guess I shouldn't be so freaked out. But it's strange, you know—" She paused. "Right, I mean, it's creepy. I get home and there's this pie."

A pause.

"Blueberry. My favorite. And he left me a note. Hold on, let me get it."

The bed exhaled and then she walked to the kitchen. A few moments later, she returned. "Dear Eliza," she read. "Please take this as an apology for what happened between us. I'd like to explain what I did and what's happened since then. What you said to me as I was saying goodbye is true: we do have a connection. I would like to rebuild it. If you don't, I understand, but please know I'm ready if you are."

She paused. "So what do you think?" she asked.

After a long pause, she said, "Let me text him. I'll call you later. Oh, by the way, how are you?" she said. I could hear some distant voice on the phone but couldn't make out the words. "Thank you. I didn't mean to make this call all about me. I just didn't know what to think!" There was a pause. Then some laughter. "I know, right!" And one final laugh. "I'll call you back. Bye. Love you."

She texted me again: "So what happened to you?"

A few responses occurred to me. "I've met with my therapist more often," came to mind, but for obvious reasons I decided not to mention that, even though it was true. My therapist had convinced me that, while Eliza was beautiful and smart and an all-around great catch, she had chosen me, a young, gainfully employed, not-half-bad-looking single guy who was unable to see the good in himself. So I settled on this reply: "Would you meet me at El Cerro Grande tonight?"

The wooden bed frame creaked as she rose again. I moved the blanket aside and saw her standing beside the kitchen table. Her brown hair was tied up and she wore a tank-top and running shorts—her Zumba outfit. With a fork she carved out a chunk of pie and then slowly raised it to her mouth. As she chewed, she closed her eyes, as if her response depended on the quality of the pie.

I covered up my hiding spot again and waited.

"I love the pie," she texted.

"I'm already in town, if you'd like to meet now."

Her footsteps shook the floor as she returned to her bed. "I felt so sad when you walked out," she wrote a moment after returning to bed. Now comes the anger.

"I'm sorry," I wrote. "I was so stupid."

"Maybe, but maybe you weren't. I need context." That's Eliza—everything needs context. "I don't know what it's like in your mind."

I was thinking of a reply when she sent another message: "And I want to know. I miss you."

"I miss you too."

"I wish I could see you right now," she wrote.

"Meet me at El Cerro Grande," I wrote. "Or wherever you want. Just name the place and I'll meet you there."

A moment later the answer came. "I'm in no condition to go out. I just finished Zumba and I'm a mess. Come back here. I'll cook something."

"I'm not sure that's a good idea."

"Why not?"

"It's an emotional place for me," I lied. In fact, under any other circumstances, I'd have loved to be there.

"I'd rather not go out tonight," said Eliza. "Just know that you can come here anytime."

That was all I needed—solid proof that what my therapist told me was true. Eliza had strong feelings for me. I *was* good enough. And yes, maybe she would someday break it off with me, but then again, maybe she wouldn't—who can control that? In that moment, I believed my therapist's wise words: Love involves risk, but it's worth it. So I held in my mind all the signs of her affection and replied: "All right. I'm coming." Then I moved the blanket aside and shimmied out from underneath her bed.

When she saw me, a look of disbelief crossed her face. Her green eyes studied me as if I had invaded earth from a distant universe. I opened my mouth to explain—and that's when she screamed.

I began hearing words come out of my mouth, explanations, all of them reasonable, if only she would listen, if only the context were still important to her, but her screams became louder and louder, and she pointed toward the door. "Out, get out! Fucking creep!" But what hurt, what really hurt me, was that she looked at me as if I were there to hurt her, to hurt her *again*, when all I wanted was the love I nipped in the bud. Her green eyes widened as if she'd just learned something new about me. But everything she was learning was wrong, and I was learning that I didn't know Eliza as well as I had thought.

VIA DOLOROSA

Matt Nestor

The purple dusk was giving way to night and, still, the scattered lamps were dark. In the dingy, rutted yard, half-buried in trash bags and teeming with rats, my cell phone screen gave the only light. The message, "I'm here," sat waiting on the screen; my finger traced figure-eights in the air above the "send" button. It wasn't too late to get a motel. Though geographically near to loony bin New Orleans, Baton Rouge is a thoroughly conventional city, and amid the endless short-grassed suburban lots, I had spotted a Super 8, a Ramada, and other peddlers of cheap, predictable sleep. A warm, drowsy evening in a warm, familiar room, takeout from WaffleHouse, and sports on the cable: all this I could have, plus a bath, and for no more than $79 and tax.

The creak of hinges, and a square of light erupted above the courtyard. A tall, bearded figure, silhouetted in a doorway that seemed to hover, called down to me.

"Matt? Is that you?"

"Robert?" I asked.

"Well, don't just stand there lollygagging. Come on up if you're ever gonna."

The matter was settled. I locked the bike, undid the panniers, and slowly climbed the stairs to the utter stranger's apartment.

*

It had been about a year since Rachel Miller turned me on to Couchsurfing.org. "You love meeting new people!" she said, grinning wildly from beneath bright-pink bangs. "It's perfect for you. We'll make an account right now."

This business about loving to meet new people was sheer projection on her part—if I am in any way a social butterfly, then she's a full-blown shark—but there were obvious upsides to the site, free accommodation being the first. It seemed too good to be true: you type in the city you're going to, message likely-looking hosts, and wait to be invited over. Not a penny changes hands: "I won't mind if you came to stay for a while," wrote Robert, a law student at LSU, and that was that.

It was only now, on the verge of meeting my first host, that I began to wonder why. As in, "*Why* won't he mind if I stay with him?" "*Why* invite a stranger to your house?" "*Why* couldn't he have picked someone he knew already, an acquaintance, say, or a distant cousin, for his sadistic, cannibal experiments?"

I lingered near the door, scanning the room for knives, garrotes, and other common torture devices. It was hard to distinguish anything amidst the rubble. To call Robert messy would be like calling Stalin disagreeable: there were enough beer bottles lying around to set a hobo up for life. Ubiquitous cigarette ash put one in mind of Pompeii, though the old takeout containers were more reminiscent of the mycology lab. Besides the sheetless bed, shared under God knows what arrangement with his friend Jerome, two reclining chairs—blue, faded, and as hard as playground slides—constituted the furniture. It gave me a pretty healthy pang to realize that Robert expected me to sleep on one of them.

Overnight arrangements aside, I had to confess Robert a congenial host. He was a Southern Gentleman: I could tell. There was his accent, for starters, slow, drawled, and thick as sofa foam. Understanding him was a process of acclimatization. Like a hiker on Everest, I started small, one word at a time. He displayed a big pink pill to me and I pointed to it and asked, "What's that?"

"Heydurul"

"What?"

"Ayderall."

"Oh," I said with dawning insight. "Isn't it awfully late? It's almost 11:00 p.m."

"Yeah," he said and shrugged his shoulders as if it couldn't be helped. He crushed the pill with the flat of a bus pass, diced it into a fine powder, and offered me a line. That was the other reason I could tell he was a Southern Gent—his innate generosity. He had already given me three bottles of Corona, and it pained him when I rejected the drugs. He snorted up half and offered the rest to Jerome.

"Damn," said Jerome, "I didn't know you wanted to go balls deep on that shit."

Robert looked at him with contempt. "Suck it up, boy."

We grabbed some road beers from the fridge and got into Jerome's improbable car. The VW Bug doesn't exactly scream "Southern," yet Jerome hailed from the same Podunk, Louisiana town as Robert. We drove around aimlessly, ogling girls and plunking stop signs with bottle caps, then decided to hit up a classmate named Gatsby for more drugs.

"I don't have any dealings with this kid unless I'm buying Xannies," Jerome explained. Observing me scribbling down what he said, he politely flipped on the overhead light. "Put this in your book: Gatsby is a retarded ass sniffer."

"Hush," said Robert. He had just dialed Gatsby on the phone.

"Hey, what are you doing? Sleeping? Sell us some Xanax real quick." Pause. "No, you come down here, we're in the Bug." He covered the mouthpiece and said to Jerome, "He says we should go meet him."

"Fuck 'im. Make him come down here," said Jerome. "I don't like that kid."

We waited five minutes, but Gatsby never showed, and we drove off. Jerome said they didn't generally do hard drugs, but since they were on probation for marijuana possession, they had no choice. "Pills don't show up in your piss test like weed does."

The road beers proceeded down our throats until none were left. Speeding on the straightaways, slowing up at corners where cops were known to lurk, we made it to a bar and chased the girls around, then dashed out again, reaching the CVS exactly three minutes before they stop selling beer in Louisiana. Back at Robert's place, we strode around the room with our fingers in each other's faces, brimming with vigorous political assertions.

It was I who noticed Jerome's phone light up. A girl we met at the bar had texted him: she "wanted his help getting high." Since they were on probation, this seemed like a bad idea, but only to me. In minutes, the boys had rushed out into the night, as eager for new and better kicks as Dean Moriarty and Sal Paradise. They could keep them. I crawled into the filthy bed and slept soundly until the boys crashed in at dawn.

"Did you get with her?" I asked Jerome, struggling to see through the gauzy sleep deposits in my eyes.

"I made out with her, but that's it. Fucking waste of time." He was on the bed, sitting where I had been, stripping off his shoes and socks. Robert hadn't bothered. Jeans still on and sweatshirt too, snores fluttering the fringes of his beard, he was already deep in slumber.

"I think I'll go and get a bite to eat," I announced. "Any diners around here?" "Yeah," said Jerome and closed his eyes.

*

By the third coffee, I was thinking logically again. And, logically, if all my Couchsurfing hosts were like Robert, then I was going to die. I had planned my entire three-month trip around Couchsurfing: if it wasn't a drunk-driving accident, or an "Ayderall" overdose, then sheer exhaustion would claim me.

Like a lab rat offered beer every time it tried to sleep, I would simply lose the will to live.

What then? I couldn't afford to stay in a motel every night. Perhaps I ought to go home and ask for my job back at the bike shop? A sort of wrenching nausea in my gut told me that that wouldn't do. One other host had accepted my request to stay with him in Baton Rouge. If he sucked, OK: I would buy a tent and sleep by the side of the road. Anything would be better than one of Jerome's blue plastic reclining chairs.

But Jeremy didn't suck. He was a comfortable person with a comfortable couch in a comfortable house. What made him especially comfortable was the flu that kept him bedridden my entire visit. I had the run of his rooms. I used his razor and ate his frozen peas. When he finally roused himself to hang out with me, we watched a basketball game on the TV. He wasn't like Robert at all. He was quite boring.

The three months went by. I visited thirteen states and stayed with about twenty-five Couchsurfing hosts. Not one killed, raped, or robbed me. Don't get me wrong: some were god-awful. There was Alison in Atlanta, who got drunk and tried to mount me in the bowling alley. There was Rachel in South Carolina, who kept her profession a secret until, a little after three a.m., she and a client had a "business meeting" in the room next mine. And there was Tony in Connecticut, that fiend, who cornered me in his room and *read me his poetry*.

But. Who are the hosts that I tell people about at parties? Who are the hosts I'm writing about now? Couchsurfing may not, in fact, be for "people who love to meet new people." Couchsurfing is for people who love to meet loons. Call it an inverse travel aesthetic: the more intolerable the accommodation, the more ludicrous the host, the happier we are. Maybe not right then, right there, the moment after the dog has pissed all over our belongings and our host, trying to help, is drowning our backpack in soda water. That's not so great. But later, much later, as we recall for our friends just how foul the piss smelled: those are sweetest moments. When we travel, we are setting by a store of experiences, to be uncorked and savored on blank days at home. Too much comfort betrays the vintage. It is misery that makes a memory piquant.

SHUTTERBUGS

David Hagerty

The call came in half an hour before closing: ". . . man down in The Wave . . ." was all the woman said before her phone cut off. I was surprised she'd gotten out even that much. The backcountry of our state park was so remote, reception was wind dependent. Since I couldn't call her back, it meant Ranger Rick was off to a rescue.

Seniority should have let me delegate this snipe hunt, but my colleagues were both busy. Stan was at the reception desk explaining to a Slavic couple, for whom English wasn't yet a second language, that the campgrounds were full and that they'd need to drive the hour into town and pay for a cheap motel, rather than stopping at the roadside and popping up a dome next to the signs with a red-slashed tent. Meanwhile, Lauren was already twenty miles out, sweeping the slot canyon of stragglers. Like khakied security guards, we had to lock down the place at sunset; except, instead of patrolling 2,000 square feet, we had as many miles. So it fell on me to help the poor tourist who'd probably tired hiking two miles to a lookout. Such mishaps were everyday, but I grabbed a first aid pack just in case.

On the drive out—five miles along a dirt road reduced to rattling washboard by too many speeding SUVs—I noted the usual array of infractions: a spit-shined pickup resting in a dry wash where even a slight rain would carry it away in a flash flood; kids crawling over Petroglyph Rock, palming the carvings left a thousand years; tourists staking out Sunset Pointe to mimic our brochure's cover shot of rocks so red they glowed like embers (unconscious that the photo was taken by a professional using a half dozen filters). For most of them, our little state park was a warmup to Zion and Grand Canyon, but for me it was a cool down on the trudge to retirement.

There were only three vehicles parked at the trailhead to the Wave, so I prayed for a quick rescue, shouldered my pack, and hiked in. I tried to hurry so I could get home for "Jeopardy" and leftover rabbit stew, but little things distracted me: the prickly pear was in bloom, with bright pink squash blossoms popping from its spiny ears; then a Chuckwalla lizard ran past, its ringed tail twitching.

The trail led downhill into an arroyo of red rock and sandstone. Half a dozen footprints headed into the black crust of the mesa, which takes centuries to repair itself; no way to tell if they were my caller's. Close by, a teenaged girl posed in a sandstone tube as her beau directed her to slide farther into the nook where rattlesnakes liked to slumber.

"You two see an injured hiker?" I said.

They paused long enough for the model to shake her head and simper after she dislodged a cascade of debris.

Past there, the path traversed slick rock and was marked by cairns. The piles were spaced every twenty-five yards to make it obvious, but people still got lost, meaning my rescue could be anywhere. Since my caller said The Wave, I followed the trail for its last quarter mile. A geologic quirk of Navajo sandstone pushed up into a rip curl, it was a favorite of photographers for its sea swirls of red and white iron ore. After cresting the final rise, I saw a trio of shutterbugs swimming in it.

"Anybody hurt?" I called.

"Down here," a woman yelled.

Ten feet below the breaker, a man lay on his side, one leg twisted improbably under him, a camera hanging from his neck like a dog tag. He was a barrel cactus, round and squat, with quills for hair and skin burnt to crust. Kneeling beside him was a pretty city gal in flip flops and a gauzy dress, the hem stained by red dust. Under a straw hat, her skin was as pale as his was red, and her hair as soft as his was coarse.

"What happened?" I said.

"I got bushwhacked," the man said. "Somebody snuck up and pushed me over the ledge when my back was turned."

While I checked his injuries, the woman stroked his hand absently, her wedding ring glinting in the fading light. Add a little makeup and I would have thought she was his daughter, but the sun had cracked her lips, and her squint brought out worry lines. Like my ex-wife, the desert was hard on her.

I couldn't find any fractures or blood on my victim, but his knee wouldn't work the same for a few weeks, and he wasn't walking out on his own. Since I didn't feel like porting a man my size alone, I squawked my radio until both Stan and Lauren picked up.

"I could use a second," I said.

"I've got an abandoned car here," Lauren said.

"Yeah, me too," Stan added.

In other words: "This one's yours."

Above, the shutterbugs were clicking away obliviously. Even after I climbed back up the ledge, they were too engrossed in their viewfinders to notice me. I had to summon them with a casual "folks."

"That man's going to need an evac," I said. "Who can help carry?"

The three kept a conspiratorial silence until a babe in man's clothing spoke up. He'd been dressed by an overprotective mom, prepped for mountaineering with new leather boots, convertible pants, and glacier glasses.

"Can't we finish our pi-tures?" he said, lisping the word without the c.

Instead of answering, I waited for the others to speak, but they were all good army grunts, volunteering for nothing.

"First tell me what happened."

I turned to a second man outfitted in a safari vest holding

a dozen lenses. His tan ran many layers deep, and his hair was bleached toward white, though I couldn't separate sun damage from age. Based on his getup and gear, he had to be a pro, although he lacked the $10 permit we required of profit seekers.

"He slipped," said safari vest.

"Hogwash," called the victim from below.

Last, I looked to a stringy old guy with hair cut by sheep shears, tissue paper skin, and an 8x10 box camera on a tripod. I'd seen him before: a local with an off-the-grid cabin. Rumors were he'd moved to the backcountry after a bad divorce. He was always alone but seemed content with his camera for company, an Ansel Adams wannabe.

"He slipped," Ansel said.

"Liar!" said my victim.

After a silence that only the desert could sustain, the woman said, "You could have slipped."

"Somebody bull rushed me," her husband said.

"Your head was in the camera."

"I know what I felt."

With ten minutes left till quitting time, I sensed my night at home disappearing with the daylight, replaced by paperwork, ambulances, and cross examinations.

"Till I know what happened, no one snaps another frame," I said.

The shutterbugs eyed the horizon; then something clicked like a gun cocking, but it was just safari vest detaching a lens.

"We're losing light," he said.

"Your time is my time," I said.

He glanced irritably to the West, but it led only to miles of canyons and mesas.

"Officer, you see that?"

He pointed to the mountains, where a full moon lay like cream cheese on a red plate.

"In five minutes, it'll be the perfect backdrop. That kind of shot only comes once a month."

"Every 29 days," I corrected. "And it's Ranger."

He stepped forward aggressively, but his doughy body couldn't support the threat.

"I drove a hundred miles for this," he said, "and you're going to ruin it because some oaf twisted his ankle."

"You can come back."

"And camp out, and hike in, and hope for clear skies?"

"Not a frame till somebody talks."

Safari vest spread the legs of his tripod and set his own equally firm behind it.

"Why punish us?" he said. "We just want some snapshots. Isn't that what you guys always preach: leave only footprints, take only photos?"

While he stared me down, mountain boy dropped his hands to his waist and twisted in place, clutching his camera close to his body. He thought I wouldn't notice him fingering the trigger, but I learned that trick from my children playing on their cell phones.

"Don't think I won't confiscate your gear," I said.

The kid stopped spinning but eyed me resentfully, proof that, like my adult daughter, he still lived with his mother and saw her as an oppressor. Meanwhile, safari vest mounted a dented camera body onto his platform and turned it my way.

"You heard the woman," he said. "He slipped."

I looked to the ledge, where the orange blossom of a desert mallow was flattened just above my victim. Then I imagined a conversation with my director the next day: me trying to explain why I detained three people for the same crime while he thought of more remote parks to banish me.

"Let me see your cameras," I said.

"You'll give them back?" mountain boy said.

"After I see them."

Meekly, he passed me an SLR with a lens bigger than a

telescope. It held dozens of shots of The Wave. In almost every one the victim was visible, crouching to show his butt crack, standing with elbows akimbo, laying atop the rock like it was a chaise lounge. Safari vests were similar, a documentary of a stranger's movements. With the 8x10, I couldn't view the unprocessed film, but I'd bet it was the same.

"None of you caught the accident?" I said.

They all shook their heads like wary coyotes.

I jumped below again to view the victim's shots, but his were all landscapes, while the woman's point and shoot showed the desert mallow framed by red rock. Hers were the only ones of the bunch that captured the fragile beauty of the place.

"Since we can't agree, we'll walk back together," I said. "Who's my porter?"

"I'm not riding one of those mules," the victim said.

His accent had that Vegas twang of cowboy fakery. For the first time I noted his getup: hand-tooled boots, an authentic Stetson, and designer jeans. It was an urbanite's version of Western chic, unscuffed or dirtied except for the places he'd landed. I'd bet he fancied himself an outlaw because he made money selling overpriced real estate.

"You rather wait till morning?" I said.

"I can pay for my own rescue."

"You can't bribe who's not here."

"Then I'll call for an evac."

He pulled his cell phone like a gun and tried to load in a new number, but the call had no barrel to guide it. As he dialed again, futilely, I looked up to the three shutterbugs, who stood at the rock edge as static as their tripods.

"Can't we take one more pi-ture first?" said mountain boy. He held up his fat lens to prove its harmlessness.

I gave him my most stern parental glare and shook my head.

So we were stuck in a gunslinger's stalemate until the woman said "I'll help."

We bookended the victim and hoisted him between us, our arms touching behind his back. Her skin felt smooth and warm.

The others followed like mules. Ansel was most cooperative, setting a leisurely pace, his box camera thrown over one shoulder. As a local, he'd get plenty of other exposures. Safari vest huffed and dragged his feet in the dust, creating a cloud around him, while mountain boy straggled behind. I kept them all on a tether by warning that I'd already recorded their license numbers—a bluff, but an effective one.

The woman's flip flops, combined with her husband's density, made it slow going. Halfway up, she was gasping and sagging, so we rested by a clump of barrel cacti. While the victim lay against a boulder rubbed smooth by millennia of floods and winds, the others pouted separately, staring toward the horizon, now in twilight.

"Don't act so colicky," the victim said.

The others stared the other way, silent.

"Y'all got no cause to be bitter."

"You wouldn't step aside," said safari vest.

"Why should I?"

"It's professional courtesy," said Ansel. "You take turns."

"That why you ambushed me?"

Instead of answering, safari vest kicked rocks down the slope, Ansel stared dreamily at the first stars, and mountain boy obsessed over a yucca. The woman sat apart, a desert bloom among clodhoppers. When a wind gust ruffled her thin dress, she shivered.

"Let's get moving," I said. "It'll be dark soon."

"What are you going to do with us?" safari vest asked.

"Just walk," I said.

Midway up, mountain boy hooked his pants on a Beavertail cactus. He tried to shake it off, but only got more ensnared until his hand-hemmed cuffs tore, so safari vest stepped on the plant's pointy ear, crushing it under his heel. The boy looked relieved until he noticed my stare.

"Oh, crud, I didn't mean . . ."

"Just walk," I said.

Another five minutes of plodding brought us to the parking lot, which held the same three cars as before. I set the victim on a bumper, then turned and saw the whole valley glowing like a photo negative. As a distraction, I said "Guys, there's your shot."

They started firing like infantry, standing and kneeling, too impatient to set up their tripods. Even my victim hopped up for a memento. Meanwhile, I slid over to the woman, who drifted the other way alone.

"You want to tell me what really happened to your husband?" I said.

"He's not my husband."

I glanced at her wedding band, which up close was scratched and scarred.

She explained "It was my grandma's. Plus, it keeps away the jerks."

"Or discourages everyone but."

"You mean my boyfriend? He's got his good side, too. I can't think what it is right now, but I'm sure it's there."

"You could do better."

"Men always say that, but it's just a come on."

Since I couldn't think how to answer that without confirming it, I returned to the original question.

"So what happened?" I said.

"He fell."

"Fell?"

She nodded and pushed around a rock with her flip flop.

"With your help?" I said.

When she lifted her face, the skin was drawn tight over her delicate cheekbones.

"You think I pushed him?"

"Your photos," I said. "That desert mallow was right next to the ledge."

She held me with a stare and wouldn't let go.

"I didn't mean to," she said. "We just bumped."

Her eyes pooled with so much sincerity that I believed her, but I doubted he would. Such men are too prone to believe ill of others to ever see their own faults. That wasn't my worry, though. Her confession was all I needed to file away this case for good.

Once their photo cravings were sated, the three shutterbugs began packing their camera gear into their cars. Urgently, the victim hopped toward us.

"What are you fitting to do about me?" he said.

"You want me to call an ambulance?"

"I want you to arrest them!"

"For what?"

He pointed to his twisted knee as though there were no more proof needed.

"No," I said. "It wasn't them."

I looked toward his better half, hoping she'd clarify, but instead she regressed to silence. The victim eyed us like he'd discovered an infidelity, then his face turned even more red.

"Take that back," he said, "or by week's end you'll be picking up trash here."

After a pregnant pause, the woman said "Don't."

"Don't what?"

"Just . . . don't."

Now all five of us waited for her to explain.

"It was an accident," she said.

He hopped a half step closer to pin her against a boulder, but she easily sidestepped him.

"You pushed me?"

"Not pushed, bumped."

"You bumped me?"

"On accident."

He gimped in a circle, hands on his head in a migraine dance. "You're such a . . . klutz!"

Her face finally gained some color, and the shutters of her eyes closed to pinpoints.

"You're the klutz!" she said. "You stepped right on my flower, like I wasn't even there."

"I was taking pictures."

"So was I until you ruined them! You always do this: drag me to these places then act like I don't exist. Why don't you ever focus on me?"

While the rest of us did just that—imprinting her furious beauty on the plates of our memory—he moved toward the road like he planned to hobble home alone.

"Faithless as a nude model," he muttered.

The mystery solved, the shutterbugs climbed into their cars and drove off, leaving a haze of red dust. As my victim waited for some better rescuer to show, the woman stared at me with dry, unwavering eyes, but that could have just been a byproduct of the desert.

"Where's your car?" I said.

She pointed toward the dry wash where I'd seen the immaculate marooned truck, so I opened my passenger door; after a backward glance at her boyfriend, she climbed in. I figured they could use some time apart and radioed Lauren to pick him up.

During the drive she was quiet, watching the moon rise over the red landscape like a pendulum and letting the wind blow through her hair, bringing with it the scent of yellow desert marigold mixed with dust. Once the cold forced her to roll up the window, she turned and said, "It must be wonderful living out here."

"It's solitary," I said.

We didn't speak the rest of the way, but when we reached her pickup, she asked if I wanted to take her into town.

A CONVERSATION WITH SHELDON RUSSELL

Lowestoft Chronicle, March 2014

Sheldon Russell
(Photography: Bob Bozarth/Bozarth Photography)

In 2001, the Western Writers of America voted Dr. Sheldon Russell's novel, *Requiem at Dawn*, as a Finalist for Best Original Paperback. Since then, his work has been praised by *The New York Times*, received starred reviews by both *Booklist* and *Publishers Weekly*, and garnered numerous awards. His fourth novel, *Dreams to Dust: A Tale of the Oklahoma Land Rush*, was recognized as an Official Oklahoma Centennial Project and went on to win the Langum Prize for Excellence in American Historical Fiction, as well as the Oklahoma Book Award in Fiction for 2006. *The Insane Train*, the second book in his acclaimed Hook Runyon historical mystery series, was selected by *Publishers Weekly* as one of the six best mysteries of 2010, and his latest mystery, *The Hanging of Samuel Ash*, was chosen as a Finalist for the Oklahoma Book Award competition for 2013.

Recently, *Lowestoft Chronicle* tracked down Russell to discuss his historical novels and his distinctive one-armed railroad detective, Hook Runyon.

Lowestoft Chronicle [LC]: Your first novel, *Empire*, was published by Evans Publications, Inc. in 1993. This was only seven years before you retired as Professor of Fine Arts at the University of Central Oklahoma. I have heard you say that your attic is full of unpublished novels. Were you writing fiction prior to 1993, and was *Empire* the first novel you completed?

Russell Sheldon [RS]: I've been writing for many years and have always been a big reader. In fact, my doctorate was in the area of Reading Specialist. *Empire* was the first book published, but not the first book written. It was published by a regional house. The print run was small, and the distribution was limited. I carried books around in my car and did signings anywhere they'd have me. I gave presentations to every imaginable group. I learned a great deal about the writing business. While I think my writing has improved over the years, I've never regretted that experience.

Requiem At Dawn
Pinnacle Books, 2000

LC: *The Savage Trail* and *Requiem At Dawn* are a couple of truly exceptional historical novels about the American frontier. Both were published by Kensington's Pinnacle Books imprint. Was it gratifying to have *Requiem at Dawn* chosen as a finalist for Best Original Paperback in the 2001 Western Writers of America Spur Awards? On the back of this achievement, why was *Dreams to Dust: A Tale of the Oklahoma Land Rush*, your fourth novel, published by the University of Oklahoma Press rather than Pinnacle?

RS: The University of Oklahoma Press is renowned for its publications about the Southwest and has a wonderful research facility as well. It seemed a perfect fit to me. At that time, my wife, a sculptor, was operating a gallery in Guthrie, Oklahoma, the site of the first Oklahoma land run and territorial capitol. From my writing studio there, I could see the train station where thousands of people arrived in 1889 on a single day to settle the town. They staked out their lots, pitched their tents, and Guthrie was born. I knew early on that it was a book I had to write. By coincidence, I finished the book the same year as the state's centennial celebration. *Dreams to Dust* went on to be selected as an Official Oklahoma Centennial Project, received the Oklahoma Book Award for Fiction, and The Langum Prize in Historical Fiction. It's currently available in paperback as well.

When *Requiem at Dawn* was selected as a Finalist for the Western Writers of America Spur Award, I was gobsmacked, as they say. I found myself competing at the national level and in the company of seasoned and successful writers. The recognition gave me encouragement at an important time in my career. By the way, no writers are more generous with their support than those in the WWA.

The Yard Dog
Minotaur Books, 2009

LC: The Hook Runyon series has proved to be very successful, with great reviews in *The New York Times* and starred reviews from *Booklist* and *Publishers Weekly*. *The Yard Dog*, the first book, published in September 2009, was even an Oklahoma Book Award Finalist. How did you get involved with the publisher, Minotaur Books? I hear you signed a four-book deal with them.

RS: Two separate contracts of two books each, actually. Not having to develop character and plot over a four-book span did have some advantages. I was able to make each book a little more independent of the others, and I like the idea of reading a series in any order that I choose. Many of my readers feel the same way.

The Insane Train
Minotaur Books, 2010

I've been delighted by some very nice reviews. *Publishers Weekly* selected *The Insane Train* as one of the six best mysteries of 2010, and I received word just this week that *The Hanging of Samuel Ash*, the most recent Hook Runyon mystery, has also been selected as a Finalist for the Oklahoma Book Award in Fiction for 2013.

I met Daniela Rapp, my editor at St. Martin's Minotaur, at a local writers' conference and pitched *The Yard Dog* to her. Ms. Rapp, having had considerable experience in the German markets, found the subject matter intriguing. She read the manuscript, liked it, and Hook Runyon's journey began. I should add that any awards my books have received are due in large part to her keen editorial skills. In the publishing business, one quickly learns how collaborative the process really is.

LC: In the acknowledgements page to *The Yard Dog*, you credit two books with helping you write the novel: *The Barbed Wire College* by Ron Robin, (about the indoctrination program for German POWs in the U.S. during WWII), and *The Rape of Europa* by Lynn H. Nicholas (about the Nazi plunder of looted art treasures from occupied countries). Did these books help to inspire the story or had you already got a general idea for the plot beforehand? And where did the idea for Hook come from? I've heard you say that, as a youngster, rail yards, steam engines, and railroad security agents fascinated you. Your father also worked as a machinist on the Santa Fe Railway. Is that where your fascination with the railroad came from—stories he told you?

RS: I had the idea well in hand before I turned to the historical literature. The POW camp in question was only a few miles from where I grew up. At its height, it contained over five thousand German and Italian prisoners. The camp water tower still stands today. So, I had been keenly aware of the camp for many years. When it was disbanded at the end of the war, the barracks were sold to various entities around the county. One of these buildings was turned into an apartment in my hometown. In the recent past, it was torn down, and two pastel paintings were discovered inside the walls. Somehow, all these details coalesced into the plot for *The Yard Dog*. I then turned to the history books to give the story as much credibility as possible. Both of these nonfiction books are particularly good accounts of the period.

My interest in railroads was inevitable, I suppose. The town I grew up in existed only because it was a division point for the Santa Fe. It had a huge roundhouse and one of the largest ice plants in the United States. Everyone in town worked for the railroad. All of the men had railroad nicknames, and everyone in town called them by those names. Even our school song was *I've Been Working on the Railroad*.

I lived through the demise of the steam engine and the arrival of the diesel, which effectively made the roundhouse and yards obsolete. Both the jobs and the men were no longer needed. The diesels could go much farther and with less maintenance than the steamers. Today, the roundhouse, the ice plant, and the railroaders are gone.

My father was a machinist and used to take me to the shops, where all the tools were gigantic and all the men were covered in soot. He told stories about the antics in the yards, which were often funny and sometimes dangerous. He talked about the POWs who worked at the ice plant. As a kid, I was taken with one story in particular about a German prisoner who would walk on his hands around the ice plant deck. It's in the book.

My dad will turn one hundred in November. He's still telling railroad stories, and I'm still listening.

LC: You once said, "In my view, journeys make the best stories, and men with flaws make the best protagonists. The railroad, the caboose, and Hook Runyon all fit the bill." The prosthetic arm doesn't seem to be much of a hindrance for Hook. In fact, there are moments when the hook is useful—when he's jumping on and off of trains, during fistfights, or prying open crates he's trapped inside of. It even proves helpful during a snake attack. What made you decide to give him a prosthetic arm rather than some other handicap? And what would you say are Hook's primary character flaws?

RS: I have always thought that journeys make the best stories, not only from the reader's point of view but also from the writer's. The narrative arch, being the journey itself, is a natural and coherent scene sequence. The protagonist begins his journey as one type of person, has good and bad experiences along the way, and reaches the end of his journey as a changed person. The scenery is varied, and the chances of meeting extraordinary folks along the way are pretty good. Anyone who doubts its effectiveness only has to read *Lonesome Dove* or *Huckleberry Finn*.

Flawed protagonists are a must, in my view. Who, after all, likes perfect people? Who even knows any? So, Hook drinks a little too much, is pretty quick to drop the hat, and is known to skip out on his debts from time to time. I perhaps went a little too far in making him a chain smoker, but have since put him on the wagon, which has done little to improve his temperament. I figure it like this: making Hook human makes him fun, and as long as the readers can see his true colors when it counts, they'll forgive him and like him the more for it.

LC: Hook is a unique and memorable character and, like many readers, I love the idea of him living in a caboose. You said that the neat thing about the series is that you "can couple up Hook's caboose to Frenchy's steamer and move him to the next trouble spot. This kind of flexibility permits new situations, places, and people." It does let you easily transport Hook across America, settling for a time in places in California, Arizona, and New Mexico. One of the surprising things, for me, is that Hook always ends up back in Oklahoma and, yet, we don't see the character Runt Wallace again (Hook's sidekick from the first book). You spent much of that first book fleshing out this character, as well as Dr. Reina Kaplan, Hook's love interest. Why did you decide to keep Frenchy (the engineer) and Eddie Preston (the divisional supervisor) in all the books and do away with Runt and Dr. Kaplan?

RS: Knowing what characters to bring forward into future books is always a tough call. The one thing I don't want to do is wear out a character's welcome. I like the idea of newly minted characters that can demonstrate different sides of Hook's personality. I like to create them as well. At the same time, I need Frenchy to keep the trains running and Eddie Preston to give out the orders and drive Hook nuts. And then there's Mixer, Hook's dog, who is essential in demonstrating Hook's softer side throughout the series.

LC: There's a moving chapter in *The Savage Trail*, your second novel, where Assistant Surgeon McReynolds relives the death of his wife, Alison, who dies on the operating table while he's attempting to remove her ruptured appendix. In the case of the Hook Runyon series, there's a brief passage in two of the books where you explain what happened to his arm. Did you ever consider writing a flashback to the traumatic car accident?

RS: It occurred to me early on that Hook might have lost his arm in the war. In as much as I was writing about what was happening at home, rather than what was happening on the front, I decided against using it. Having a mind of his own, Hook has taken his disability in stride. It is part of his charm and courage. So I abandoned the idea of emphasizing it much altogether, deciding, instead, that I should not make a big deal out of something that he doesn't. There is also a certain pathos, I think, about a man of Hook's strength and sensitivity who has been left behind in the war.

LC: With *The Hanging of Samuel Ash* (Book #4) published last year, does this mean the end of the series, or is there a fifth installment in the works?

RS: The jury is currently out on that one. I have a fifth Hook Book in manuscript form, with the working title of *The Bridge Troll Murders*. Hook goes undercover as a hobo. By the way, Runt Wallace, one of my personal favorites, does, in fact, return for another Hook adventure.

LC: *The Dig: In Search of Coronado's Treasure*, published in August of last year by the University of Oklahoma Press, is a different type of historical mystery—one where two stories, one set in the past and the other in the present, are interwoven. What led you to write this stand-alone novel and why did you decide to tell the story this way? Incidentally, what made you decide to move toward historical mystery in the first place, and is your latest novel an indication that you will be continuing to write in this genre?

RS: I grew up in the Gloss Mountains of Northwestern Oklahoma, not far from where Coronado made his trek north in search of the seven cities of gold. One day, classmates brought an iron lance point to school. It was the general consensus that this may well have belonged to Coronado. As a youngster, I was intrigued by the notion that someone may have passed this way five hundred years before me.

Once an image gets stuck in my head, it's there until I have reconciled it, usually through writing. So I chose to tell two stories concurrently, one in the past about Coronado's search for the gold, the other a contemporary story about a young archeologist on a summer dig. I wanted the reader to sense the continuum of time, to feel that the past is as infinite and mysterious as the future, that we are all somehow still connected. I've always felt that Eugenides came very close to achieving this in his book, *Middlesex*.

I'm simply not sure the direction future books will take. While I've always had an affinity for the past, and love finding a nugget from history and writing about it, I'm also compelled by evil forces within me to write what I want to write. I'm aware that doesn't always make the best marketing sense, but there you have it. The writing has to be fun and interesting for me, or I can't pull it off. Here's hoping my readers will follow. I'm currently writing a psychological thriller called *Shrink Wrapped*. I rest my case.

A QUESTION OF THE TIDE

Victor Robert Lee

I say Romero should've taken a lesson from the mud crabs. They're spread out by the thousands when the tide gives them leeway in the mangroves, and if a man walks among them in the slop, all the crabs inside a four-step radius dodge into their holes. You take another step, and the next circle scats and dives. They're out again as soon as you pass, swiveling those eyes on little stalks. Wary. Smart.

This guy Romero was chatty but only in spurts, so he left me wondering if we really were chums after all. Both of us were up from Buenos Aires, *porteños* just scraping by and all that. Even solitary surfers chunk-up when they're dipping new breaks, especially in a far-gone place like this, way up from Bahia, so that's what we were doing, hanging together, getting by on Spanish even though the locals speak Portuguese. And I tell you this—what they say about Spanish and Portuguese being born of the same mother—well, one of them is a bastard. The body language is a whole other story. Romero could vouch for that.

When he did talk, Romero loved to spout off about beautiful nature this, beautiful nature that, going on and on about the little fish that swam just in front of his nose for a whole hour in the maze of the reef that shelters this stretch of coast. No normal wave raker goes in for that sentimental stuff. We've got one thing on the brain. Not Romero, and he paid for it.

It all started when he had to chuck the board a few days after we met, when I clipped him on a niner tube I didn't want to share. Greedy bastard, that's me, and famous for it. Maybe that's why only a Romero could put up with yours truly.

But shit, I didn't mean for him to take that rip on the reef. A better man would've slapped shallow. He didn't. Probably daydreaming about the guppy on his nose. So Mister Hairy Reef took a chomp on Romero's chest. I helped him back to the sand, blood streaming out. Some old nurse, maybe just a seamstress, sewed him up, and the color came back to Romero's face. Never said a bitchy word about it. Problem was, the bite was on the ribs that met the board when he paddled. So oops, no more surfing this trip.

Believe this? He said he'd pay for chow at a shack on the beach that night. I wondered if he was going to sprinkle cyanide on my crab when I went for a pee, but when I came back, he was talking to a big man and his woman who'd sat at our little table. Big Guy, called Sergio, was freckly white, could've been one of those Irish rugby players you see on TV. His babe was brown and slim—looked Italian to me, but turns out they were both natives. That's Brazil. They kissed while we cracked the crabs and shoveled bits of octopus.

The waitress wasn't much, so I kept my eyes on Marisa, Sergio's wife or who-knows-what, trying to catch a look. No go. But the way Romero told it, even while Sergio and Marisa were lip-to-lip, Marisa was pressing her bare feet against Romero's in the sand. Even poking her toes in the gaps between his. I would've thought that was an invitation for a threesome, but Sergio didn't seem to be in on the party. Romero's not bad-looking, sure, but Marisa could've poked her little piggies my way. Now I'm glad she didn't.

They made Romero show his wound with all the stitches. Big deal. Marisa even touched and tickled the scabby edges of the slice, both sides. Romero broke another crab and asked Sergio to tell us about the spear fishing. Sergio was a bragger. Had such-and-such kind of double-outboard fiberglass skiff with this-and-that gear like we're supposed to care, and the precious boat was hidden in a secret spot up the estuary where only he could find it, better there than at the dock where the village lackeys would steal it. Then he got on about all the fish he'd speared two days before, sizes and types and how they fought. While he's showing his perfect aim like he's going to shoot the waitress over at the grill, I see Marisa's hand go beneath the table and I'm sure it was on Romero's leg or worse because Romero dropped a pink claw and gave some attention to Sergio's aim. But I could swear that a second later that bastard Romero had shifted in his chair to get a little closer to Marisa. Might've been rubbing his knee against hers; who knows? All I can say is, I started concentrating on which way Sergio's eyes were pointed too. Just when he turned back from the imaginary hunt, I knocked the table leg with my heel. Two beers went down, one gushing onto Sergio's lap. He didn't seem to catch what was going on, only started singing some tune about spilled beer and the romance that always followed and wrapped Marisa in his big arms until she seemed to disappear. Sergio ended up paying the whole tab; said he liked surfers and hoped he could learn to hit the waves himself someday.

The way Romero told it, next day he bumped into Marisa and Sergio on the beach road. Sergio stopped his black pick-up truck and asked if Romero needed a ride to town. Marisa opened the door and let her leg dangle out. Romero said no thanks, he'd hoof it, take in the nature. Nature, sure—Marisa's lean leg for instance, that's what I'da been thinking. But Sergio took him at his word and said he and Romero should go fishing the next day since the wound meant his surfing was busted. He said there was lots of *nature* in the blue at the far edge of the reef, and that no doubt Romero was a fucking good swimmer, and the season was right, and he's got two spearguns, he needs to give the outboards a run anyway to keep them healthy, and the tide will be up just after breakfast. Helluva pitch from Sergio—damn well thought-out, if you ask me. And I wonder if Romero was interested because he thought Marisa would be fishing too. I gotta be honest here: Marisa was tasty to the eye. If she'd put her sandy toes on mine, I'd be in the same fix.

Anyway, Romero agrees to go fishing.

Morning. There was action where the reef makes an underwater point before it gives way to the river mouth. I barely said a hey-yah to Romero while I was humping it toward the beach. I looked back when I was paddling out. Saw him get into that black truck. No sign of Marisa.

The way Romero told it, Sergio was all friendly and eager when they were slogging around trying to find his boat. Wasn't easy. Up this stream and the next, knee-deep in mangrove muck until they found the secret spot. Then a prop got stuck in the mud. At least he was right about the tide. They got out of the estuary and headed toward what Sergio called big game country. Big game? Why Romero didn't just dive overboard and swim back to an easy beach and easier pleasures, I don't know, and it bugs me, just like that amused look he always had on his face, as if he was in on some funny secret and there was no way he was going to share it.

First business on the boat was learning how to shoot the spear. How to cock the long rubber band, the maximum distance for a hit. Child's play, but Sergio made a big deal out of it. He said he was always proud to bring a big fish back to Marisa for dinner. She couldn't cook, but a chef in the village would make it just the way she liked it, and Marisa deserved a good fish. Always.

They put on masks and jumped in. Telling this, I'm prickly. Romero in the water with an armed man whose girlfriend has been feeling Romero up. Sure, Romero's got a speargun too. But who knows where Sergio is coming from? Rather take my chances with the sharks, and there are plenty of them here by the reef. Adds a little juice to the surfing, makes you want to hang topside as far as the wave can take you.

Water's a little murky. Sergio is ahead. He looks back at

Romero and points down. They both dive. Sergio with that big chest—I bet he could take a nap on the bottom before he'd need air. They dove a few times, missed on two shots, and reloaded at the surface. Out of the blue, Sergio says his gal is hot, right? Romero thinks about this, then says everybody's got their own thing. Sergio says you mean she's *not hot*?

Right here I'm thinking of that species of woman who tries to seduce you, and if you don't join in, she'll tell her man you've tried to get between her legs and you're fucked either way. But this being the southern hemisphere, it's all upside down, and it's the man who's trying to trip you up.

Romero spiels it like a diplomat, says that all Brazilian women are hot, that's why everyone comes to Brazil. So she's *hot, right*? Sergio says again. Romero admits it: Marisa is fucking hot. What do you mean *fucking* hot? I mean, you're a lucky man, Romero says. Sergio isn't satisfied with lucky. Think I got her by luck? I worked on her since she was fourteen. Made her have my bed. A virgin. Call that luck? Call that *luck*?

Two guys bobbing up and down, treading and talking like this—the water can be rough outside the reef. You pump your legs and sweep your one free arm to keep your mouth above the waves. And Romero's got to think fast at the same time, poor sucker.

You call that luck? Sergio wants an answer. I have *bad* luck, says Romero. Probably thinks he's pulling a rabbit out of a hat with this one: He says the cut on his chest is bleeding again. Time to go back to the boat.

Sergio says, don't worry, he'll shoot any shark that comes, and thanks for being the bait. He looks down through his mask at the strings of blood coming from Romero's chest and says this is real hunting. Never speared a shark before. Marisa will love eating it with moqueca sauce.

The way Romero told it, Sergio meant what he said about the shark hunting—kept himself between Romero and the boat, with the speargun not aimed at Romero, but not too far off target either. Come on, the hunt's just beginning, says Sergio, give it a little time; I won't let them chew on you. We're fishing buddies. And I'm a damn good shot.

Romero's cut is wide open and leaking more. I'd seen it when he got clipped, and it was deep like a hatchet had landed there. He'd just pressed a hand on it till we found the seamstress. Tough guy for a nature lover.

Romero tries to angle off, wide of the reef, toward the river mouth, thinks he'll just skip the boat and swim back. But Sergio swims with him, and now they're doing water ballet right where the grays like to feast—where the fresh water meets the salty sea.

Sergio keeps up his buddy-buddy talk, says they'll be heroes in the village when he and Romero motor in with a shark and pull it up on the dock. And then he says... He's shouting over the rocking water when he says: Marisa will *love* us if we get this shark. She'll *love* us.

*

Romero sort of lost track of things after that—his memory of the whole thing is full of potholes. Next thing he recalls is dragging Sergio across the mangrove mud with the crabs running to their tunnels. Sergio's left arm was missing, but Romero'd managed to squeeze the stump with the diced-up rubber band from Sergio's speargun before he pulled the big guy through the rooty tangle.

Here's where I come in. Sergio is lying in the little clinic. The shark had laid some teeth into his hip too, but I guess it hadn't been big enough to make him a meal. Arm gone, hip chewed, some scrapes to the face. Bunch of village folks are huddled around, saying last month's case was worse. Romero is there, muddy pile on the floor.

Sergio is in and out of it, eyes every which way. Marisa

struts in. Sergio comes to. He starts howling and wailing and telling her how much he loves her, begging to know if she feels the same. Begging and begging. Marisa puts a hand on his face and strokes his mucky hair. Shush, shush, she says. You're a strong man, a real man. You'll be all right. Sergio tries to reach for her with his one arm but he's too weak. You love me? He goes on with the begging. You love me? You love me? All she says is let them put the bandages on and I'll drive you to the big hospital. Then I'll take you home. She keeps stroking him and stroking him. Never looks at Romero and me. I'm happy for that.

I pull Romero up to his feet. I'm thinking Sergio and his woman are lost somewhere in the tidal zone on a shore break— high tide is love, low tide is hate. Maybe vice versa. Between them is where you can get the best ride, if the swell is strong and the wind is right and... Hell, what am I talking about? Love? Me?

Outside the clinic door it's too bright, and Romero feels too heavy on my shoulder, like he's passing out. But then, when I've sat him down to drink a squeeze of *maracujá* at a street stall, Romero perks up. He tells me Sergio saved his life. Shot the shark just in time, then the thing turned on Sergio. Romero wants to go back and tell that to Marisa.

Saved his life! I laugh. Romero tries to get up, but I shove him back down, and it's a good thing he's still too beat because I'll tackle him if he tries to go back there. Saved your life? I say. I pull off my T-shirt and wad it up, press it against the weepy reef bite on his chest. And while I'm handing him more juice, I'm thinking Romero shouldn't have let me steal that niner tube, shouldn't have been daydreaming about the guppy on his nose, shouldn't have gone fishing, and I'm telling myself it's all his fault.

BANGKOK OF THE MIND

Stephen Cloud

Having strayed from his purpose
Owle steeled himself and crossed the city,
a maze of stinks, non-negotiable and overwhelming.
But by now he had lost the capacity to feel
overwhelmed. He took everything in stride
though his stride was more like a bleary stagger
down blind streets and through wild warrens:
Patpong Road, the night market where the din
of bargain offerings came at him in yelps and coos,
persistent, seductive, mystifying.
It would take him days to reach the bitter end
of Bangkok—days and nights, incessant wandering,
mile after mile of ill-lit hovels, fires in oil drums,
stalled traffic, a melee of taxis and motorbikes,
tuk tuks and lorries loaded down with contraband.
But it had to be this way: Bangkok. Aimless wandering.
He was cutting to the chase now, penetrating,
discovering for himself the entry point
of the eight-fold path, the first principles,
the sine qua non, the mission that meant everything:
going deeper to the source, elusive and reeking,
of the rot that had been destroying him inside and out.

THE CAMBODIAN VOID: AN APOLOGY

Soren A. Gauger

The Devil knows what I put in my mouth, but it immediately made me feel sick. There were five or six of them skewered on a stick; they had spindly little legs, and it was clear from how the Cambodians were watching me that I was eating them the wrong way. Endangering my health, Or just being vulgar. You never could tell with these Cambodians and their expressionless faces; they could watch you drink carpet cleaner without batting an eyelid.

And their suits, those incompetent replicas of long-outmoded Western fashions, and their hair, invariably cropped so that it stood on end. Sopheap, the shorter of the two, had a pock-marked complexion and the infuriating habit of laughing extravagantly at his own mindless humor. Munny had the cruel demeanor and hair-trigger temper typical of very skinny men. He compulsively chewed the sunflower seeds he kept loose in the pockets of his polyester suit. They were always exchanging glances so filled with sadism and treachery that the skin crawled. I kept imagining them a pair of giant iguanas, hunched over the table and silently blinking their eyes.

I've made the corrections to the contract, I said, pulling it from my briefcase, removing it from the protective plastic envelope, and pushing it across the table toward them. I had overlooked, somehow, a puddle of brown sauce; the contract slid right through it, and as Cambodian restaurants are never supplied with napkins, I was left to wipe at it with the sleeve of my tailor-made shirt.

Now you have sauce contract, howled Sopheap, sauce contract! He opened his mouth wide and laughed for a terrifyingly long time, exposing his rotten, crooked teeth, fastening me with his steely eyes, and only after a full minute of this did I forfeit the last of my dignity and laugh along. He sat back, satisfied, resuming a blank expression.

Munny picked up the soggy papers, studied them for a moment, and said: Of course, we not sign this. This no good. And he slid the papers back across the table to me.

Little beads of sweat popped to the surface of my forehead and the backs of my shoulder blades. I registered that it was hot, fiendishly so, that the outside of the restaurant was crowded with some bizarre, muscular species of dog, that the music had a hypnotic undertow which was making it difficult to think clearly.

Well, but that's precisely why, I said, forcing a confident smile and ramming the contract back into the plastic sleeve, that's precisely the reason why I have here prepared an identical copy of the document, I said rifling through my briefcase, a second...

But just as the words left my lips, I had a sudden flash of the documents sitting on the bureau of my hotel room, right alongside the mini-bar, and I looked up to meet the blank stares of my associates.

It's a minor setback, I told them, my voice drained of self-assurance, absolutely a minor setback. This is an absolutely run-of-the-mill kind of, I coughed, obstacle. As I continued to babble similar nonsense, my mind spun with snapshot memories of the past ten days, of ingratiating the stupid and patently irrational whims of these Cambodian reptiles, toasting them with glass after glass of rice wine, accompanying them to sleazy dives covered with mirrors and black enamel tabletops so that the waitresses whom, Sopheap had informed me with a grin, knew how to reward a big tipper, could charge you Hong Kong prices for the shoddy replica of luxury. I had flattered their acumen, though I knew the rhetorical subtleties of my compliments to be beyond them both linguistically and culturally, I had ordered them—and myself, alas—a gourmet soup called *kokhiya sâmlâ*, from whose murky green depths one fished out revolting surprises with a spoon. I had pandered, compromised, laughed at jokes I found either moronic or vulgar, or which I simply didn't understand. I realized I had come to expect from them less intelligence than I would credit a wild animal. Most distressingly, however, I had begun to sense, as I looked into the black depths of their eyes, that they were looking at *me* with the very same annihilation of personhood and identity, the same void I experienced when I looked at them. We were obliterating each other, I realized, turning each other into single-cell creatures, and there was not a blessed thing any of us could do to stop it, things had progressed too far. And after a few days, I had even found that it stayed with me, this sense of the void within me; I wandered about with it inside my gut; it became the vantage point from which I apprehended the world, and my own actions in it.

Waiter! I cried, Bring these men two bowls of *kokhiya sâmlâ*. I shall return in half an hour, I told them, I've just left it in my hotel. Please! Don't move.

I kicked my way past the stray dogs, slapped away a few beggars, and made it to my rented car, once a shining symbol of foreign wealth, now coated in a layer of Cambodian grime. How can they expect people to behave *normally* in this country, I thought, if wherever you go you get covered in filth, if a man has to walk through his entire life in dirt? Small wonder they're belligerent, it could scarcely be any other way. It was my last night to close the deal before my plane left for Moscow the following morning, and from there on to Odense, where my idiot employer, Mr. Nielsen, was waiting in his crisp, sterling, 21st-century office, with every modern convenience, as they say, at his fingertips. As I climbed into the car, I remembered how he had poured me some fine Scottish whiskey, and his soothing baritone voice had said: Do whatever you please with these people. None of our company policies or ethics stretch as far as Cambodia. Nothing you do there has any *real* repercussions at all. As you know, here in Denmark, and in this office in particular, we have a great many *stringencies*. Often we don't understand why these rules could possibly be good for us, but we do our best to abide by them anyway. All those things you can leave in your cubicle before you go. All your niggling little doubts, your good breeding—tipping waiters, please and thank-you, chivalry, subtlety, savoir faire, even the most basic hygiene—all of this I want you to leave here in Odense. I will tell you a secret. Your manners won't merely go unnoticed, they will even trip you up, slow you down. These people will respect you *less* for your politeness. They take it as a sign of weakness. I know it sounds incredible, but believe me, I have had years of experience with these savages. I may not yet fully understand the heart and mind of the Cambodian, but I do know that he will eat you alive if you stroll in with European good graces.

The car jolted strangely and clattered to a halt. Street urchins seized the opportunity to cluster around, trying to sell me what appeared to be a tiny human fetus floating in a jar. I swiped at it with my hand; the vile thing went crashing to the street, spraying the side of the car with a thick vitreous fluid. I rolled up the window and the car sped off, leaving the urchins shaking their fists in its wake.

...already mentioned, *there is no game plan*, Nielsen resumed, out in Cambodia, except this: bring me back the contract with those signatures. They will do everything in their power to delay this, even though, insanely enough, they honestly believe the contract to be in their best interests. It is simply there in their blood. They love to make the foreigner linger, through increasingly base and unscrupulous methods. These people are in constant pursuit of the inane. This much was true, I now recalled from inside the automobile, what had I been doing for these past ten days? I had been urging myself deeper and deeper into the Cambodian psyche, shucking off layer upon layer of Danish breeding and dignity in bars, conference rooms, public toilets, looking into a series of mirrors, each time a bit more grizzled and misused, my ironic detachment turning into something quite different, much more difficult to put a finger on, a kind of oceanic frailty, a total evaporation of confidence at what this gradual whittling of my identity would bring, or in turn build, if all of this *erasure* did not, at least in some abstract sense, have its equal and opposite reaction, to which I was not attending in any conscious—

A sickening thwack. The car jolted to a stop. My head hit the dashboard.

I came to—it couldn't have been more than a few seconds—with a great dizziness, and the pulse of my lips throbbing against my teeth. I wiped my mouth with my sleeve, and registered, though only faintly, that it left a long streak of blood. Well, that's fine, I thought, or said out loud, nothing a few ice cubes couldn't fix, maybe a—I caught a glimpse of my own face in the rear-view mirror and a shudder ran through my bones. I'll just have to give the face a quick scrub as well, nothing amiss there. I checked out my limbs, and found them all to be in fine working order, with the possible exception of a slight twitch in the right leg. I eased myself out of the car, the crunch of broken glass underfoot, a stabbing pain in the buttocks when I walked.

And irrelevantly I thought—it wasn't for this my parents put me through Harvard, it wasn't for this, surely, that I stayed up nights poring over economics textbooks, learning Russian, German, Chinese; in fact, bits of everything except Khmer. It wasn't for this that I learned, step-by-step, how to seduce a young woman from a good family, flattering her beauty exactly no more or less than her intelligence, keeping my baser thoughts to myself. It wasn't for this, was it, that I had worked my way into the trust and open arms of three successive corporations, exploiting my boyish good looks and what I had come to accept as my natural charisma? And now the madness of it all! The total, maddening incongruity with the pathetic, crippled, Cambodian picture I now presented. Now rein yourself in, I thought, time to focus on the reality at hand, however vulgar it may be.

In Cambodia, it never takes more than a few seconds for a crowd to form. They were all gathered around the front of the car. I had escaped everyone's attention, and so I abandoned the car, its door wide open, and slipped off, crossing the street, walking at a diagonal slant. I had made it less than a hundred feet when I heard a woman break into a wailing shriek. Well, I thought, something dreadful must have happened in conjunction with the car, best not to look back, and I hobbled a bit faster, hooking right into a department store.

The entrance aisle was lined with mannequins on pedestals; because this was Cambodia, many were missing fingers or noses, the shapes of their bodies exuded a rank sexuality, and their clothes were ill-fitting and shabby—the effect was a row of beggars and war veterans, stooping over to take a coin. A white man can never melt into a crowd in Cambodia, I reminded myself, passing through these grotesqueries, but perhaps I can find a rear exit, then creep through the back alleyways, make it to my hotel that way.

I slunk past a man demonstrating how deftly a kitchen knife sliced through something that might have been an eggplant, had it not been orange and filled with a thick syrup, swung left toward the menswear department, passing rows of leather jackets, reflecting on how the Cambodians were helplessly seduced by leather and gold, like all the downtrodden and uncultured peoples of the world. I approached a little fat man piling shoeboxes in a corner.

I grabbed him by the shoulder. Firmly now, I thought.

Look here, I said, I can't give you *all the details*, but the situation, just between you and I, is *urgent*. Have you got a supply entrance I could just slip through? Could you do this simple thing for me?

He was staring at my face all the while, with a pathological steadiness, but he made no response, not a word, not the slightest expression or gesture. How else to get through to this vegetable? And here, again, I found myself confronted by the void, staring deep into it and, therefore, deep into the vacuity of my own soul again. I was already familiar with this kind of demonism. I had spent ten whole days trying to grasp what lay behind it. Now I was bored and disgusted, sick of pretending to tolerate and understand this subhuman mode of interaction. Somebody had to start making examples of these people, chipping away at their obvious sense of impunity—starting with this goddamn shoe salesman. You do speak English, don't you, I snarled, less as a question than a command. Again, the same bland, utterly equivocal expression, the glassy eyes, shiftless as the desert sands. Hopeless, I said, you're a disaster, giving him a push to vent my rage, and stalked off, the fury mounting. Two salesmen were having a card game at the glove counter. Steady now, I told myself, one last try.

Now listen here, I said, and listen good. I'm looking for a back entrance. Unperturbed, one of them lay down another card, which his opponent calmly studied.

Look me in the face, I said, my voice becoming shrill, I need your attention. As the other man laid down a jack of clubs, my patience gave, and just as I was about to really cut into them, I had a sudden mental flash of the rear-view mirror, my blood-streaked, disfigured face, and I recognized the problem: It was me; I looked like a madman. I backed off, and in a few minutes I had found a washroom.

The Danish washroom bathes the visitor in a powerful, invigorating light. The Cambodian equivalent offers a dank, cave-like atmosphere. Nonetheless, I could make out the general outlines of my body in the mirror; I was in terrible shape, and my hands, I registered, were shaking so fiercely I could scarcely wet them under the faucet. I really would have to see a doctor when I arrived home, I decided. People in car accidents seldom recognize that they are suffering the effects of long-term shock. Remember Aunt Regina, the way she always shrieked and turned pale whenever she heard the sound of broken glass. I splashed water all over myself. The heat was most intense in the bathroom. I need to get out, I thought, loosening my tie.

I was now fairly confident I was presentable, surely no more insane looking than the average Cambodian male. I limped deep into the heart of the department store, past more knife demonstrations, leering salespeople, squinty-eyed mannequins, screeching animals in bamboo cages, pickled entrails in jars, television sets flashing catastrophes, crippled children begging for money, until I was sure that, just beyond the shimmering hills of the porcelain section, I saw the back door. I broke into a stumbly run and bounded past a table display of teapots, hooking a foot on a table leg and flying, sprawled out toward the ground. Worse, a cracking sound signified I had kicked free the table's supports. What followed had a pastoral beauty—a slow-motion hailstorm of china teapots, splintering shards dancing to-and-fro all over, everywhere, tinkling and cracking, spreading a vast mosaic of rainbow-colored broken porcelain around me—and then a teapot collided heavily with the back of my skull.

A whistle brought me back to my senses—policemen charging through the department store. Suddenly, possessed by a lucidity brighter than I had felt for days, perhaps since I had left Denmark, I rammed through the crowd to the service door, my heart pumping wildly. The door led to a landing. At the foot of the landing stood a motorcycle.

Things have come this far, I said, setting my jaw. I jumped

on the vehicle, kick-started it, the policemen's whistles bearing down on me, and I flew off at a cracking speed.

I had never driven a motorcycle previously, and found it to be quite unlike the American films. This vehicle jolted about nauseatingly on the broken paving stones, splashed through puddles of filth, scattered packs of children, monkeys, or long-necked birds, coughed a greasy black smoke, and vibrated hard enough to make my teeth shake, but it gave me a sense of euphoria such as I had never experienced in Cambodia; finally I was putting these people where they belonged, cutting through their defense shields, chasing them back into their grim little rat-hole apartments, to breed some more of their foul children, generations of broken-toothed, broken-backed—

Then suddenly the slums had evaporated, and now I was cruising past my international hotel—a typically Cambodian sort of contradiction. The clock in the hotel lobby told me that twenty-five minutes had expired since I had left Sopheap and Munny in that restaurant, an incredible compression of time, I thought, pushing my way into the elevator.

The most demonic thing I had seen yet: all the people crowded in the elevator had the same face, literally identical, their features that of an imbecile, looking forward with the same, glazed expression, into the vast Cambodian nothingness, noses pressed flat against their skulls. I swallowed a gasp. A fly nattered in the still of the elevator. There is always a fly in Cambodia, and in unison all the identical heads began slowly swiveling to face me.

The silence was utterly maddening. Something ghastly will happen, I thought, when I am confronted by all those faces at once. There was the dreadful sensation that one void was about to stare into the depths of multiple others all at once, with all the horrors this entailed, as the elevator shot endlessly up into space. We were about to enact an apocalypse in miniature, on the scale of this elevator, to the buzzing of this fly, with neither trumpets nor cloudbursts. I sank deep into myself, groping for something solid to combat the void, because if there was nothing to be done with the yawning abysses all around me, if there was nothing to be dredged from *that* blackness, then perhaps my own personality had not *entirely* abdicated, perhaps there was a shred to salvage, and I plumbed deep, but kept finding everywhere this blanket of emptiness, and the deeper I went, the more unnerving it became. As the swiveling heads were nearly upon me the policeman's whistle blew again somewhere in the distance, the elevator doors slid open, in stepped two obese Germans, and all the identical heads snapped back into their glazed neutral positions.

How did I get back in the lobby? With the spare contract in my pocket? And only two-and-a-half minutes to intercept Sopheap and Munny on their way out of the restaurant? The motorcycle, naturally, refused to kick-start, only spluttering in response to my efforts. No cause for alarm, I thought, though I knew Asiatics to be fanatically punctual, and at that moment a bus wheezed up and came to a stop before my feet. I heard another blast on the whistle from that police officer and leapt in, the doors slapping shut behind me.

What was it that came out of the crevices? I was standing in the aisle, steeling myself against the vehicle's nauseating lurch, and I noticed that the corners of my periphery were darkening. All around me slouched the same Cambodian public, oblivious as always; but now encroaching all around them, with a steady pulse, this ominous shade. Blinking my eyes was no help.

I looked up toward the ceiling and gasped. It was spreading from there, burbling outward from some unseen center-point then groping down, shadowing-forth, down the windows, even dribbling bits onto the floor. I gave the man to my left a desperate shake on the shoulder but he only turned to me with his ink-black eyes, and a shudder went through me. The bus was moving faster now, its gears making wild gnashing sounds.

I was thrown against a pane of glass.

There was no doubting it: through the window, seconds before the darkness swallowed up my view, I saw two giant reptiles stepping out of a restaurant, one nonchalantly checking his wristwatch, starting to walk away. *Sopheap!* I cried, and when the bus stopped for a red light, almost entirely swallowed in blackness, I put my foot through the window, held the contract out at arm's length, yelling: Munny! Someone stop those iguanas! The whistle now blaring, a cracking pain in my skull, and I was still shouting the same thing when I came to my senses, to find two policemen dragging me from under the arms, picking me up from the wreckage of broken porcelain, through the throngs of ogling Cambodians, past my car wreck where that woman was still wailing and cursing the skies—no sense in looking, nobody wails so inhumanly over the death of a dog—and into the back of a windowless police van, into the pure Cambodian blackness.

MY DRIVER, SUNDAY

Mona Zutshi Opubor

Two years ago, my Nigerian-American husband told me he wanted to move our family from New Jersey to Nigeria. Though I'd never lived outside the U.S., I immediately agreed to go.

After researching Lagos online, I regretted my knee-jerk marital support. Dire warnings of crime abounded. My husband assured me that we would all be fine.

John had never steered me wrong but I panicked. It was clear to me our deaths were imminent. I gave away most of my possessions and had a lawyer draft our wills.

For the record, John was right and I was wrong. No one was killed. But according to marital law, a husband must never realize he can win an argument with his wife so please do not tell him.

*

On the day we moved, our suburban house stood empty, the furniture was crammed into a shipping container at the Elizabeth seaport, and my beloved minivan sat in a lot at the dealership, for-sale signs plastered to the windows.

Our Honda Odyssey could hold two adults and five children. My kids snacked frequently and the floor was littered with fish-shaped crackers. Between the art projects they shredded on the way home from school, the crumbs, and the shrieking, it was like driving around with a frat party. Washing the minivan was pointless. It was filthy a day later.

In Nigeria, life changed.

I won't drive in Lagos. I can't. It's too scary and I'm not

equipped. I have anxiety just thinking about it. If I were ten years younger, I wouldn't be afraid. But ten years ago, I was still operating under the assumption that I could outsmart death.

*

We hired a driver named Sunday.

I ended up spending a lot of time with Sunday as we sat in traffic. Sunday talked to me and gave me advice. At least, that's what I think he was doing.

I couldn't understand a word Sunday said.

At first I asked him to repeat himself. But that didn't help. Sunday's first language is Igbo. He also speaks Pidgin. Often he listened to Pidgin radio programs. I couldn't understand those either. They sounded like Martian and then all of a sudden, the announcer would slip something in like, "Victoria Island," or "Lekki-Epe Expressway," and I would remember we weren't listening to an alien transmission.

I began to suspect Sunday understood very little of what I said, as well. But he embraced my technique of feigning comprehension, laughing heartily and nodding in agreement.

When I asked him to take me to Reddington Hospital, he took me to the Radisson Hotel. When I asked him to take me to Deli's, he took me to the American Embassy. He tried to take me to the Embassy so often that I wondered if he was suggesting I repatriate myself.

*

I began writing down addresses of places I wanted to visit. Whenever I asked Sunday to take me somewhere new, he would snatch the slip of paper from my hand and clutch his head like he had a migraine. He would mumble the street names for a few minutes. It was unclear if he was trying to plan the best route or gathering up the courage to start the car. He seemed shaken.

After some time had passed, he would begin to drive in

slow circles. After half an hour, he would ask a passing okada driver for directions. If Sunday had understood my accent, I would have suggested that he *begin* by soliciting the help of an okada driver.

When commercial motorcycles were banned in Lagos, the odds of us finding our destination plummeted.

*

Sunday enjoyed sharing his pro-Igbo viewpoint with me in regards to other Nigerian ethnic groups.

He once spoke to me at length regarding the Hausa. I couldn't understand that conversation at all. Maybe he gave me a cogent analysis of their defining traits. I have to assume not, however, based on what he told me about the Yoruba.

Sunday had the ability to blame any and all social ills squarely on the shoulders of the Yoruba people.

For example, when I told him I planned to withdraw the kids from school because the teachers had slapped them, I knew what was coming. My husband was in the car so he was able to translate Sunday's English into actual English.

"That's terrible," Sunday said. "We Igbo know how to beat children. We know there are limits. But Yoruba, they don't have limits." Sunday then claimed that Yoruba parents wake up their children every morning by beating them.

I was curious about Sunday's interpretation of current events: Were the Yoruba responsible for the European debt crisis? Did they cause the war in Iraq? Has Barack Obama been briefed on the Yoruba menace that surrounds us?

It was upsetting to hear prejudice openly discussed. I seethed on behalf of Yoruba everywhere. I am all for ethnic pride but not when it hints at ethnic cleansing.

I took comfort in the fact that I couldn't make heads or tails of most of Sunday's comments.

*

As the months passed, however, we adjusted to Lagos. I began to understand my driver's accent. We were often stuck in traffic. And to my horror, Sunday began to talk all the time.

It was torture to be marooned in a sea of vehicles while the kids fought and Sunday rambled. He broke the monotony of his chatter by crashing our SUV into pedestrians, stationary objects or other vehicles, depending on what was available.

Sunday appointed himself my life coach. At first, I wasn't troubled when he began interrupting my conversations to correct my speech. He insisted that "Chevrolet," rhymed with, "omelet." He informed me I was pronouncing my children's names wrong, which was peculiar. I am Indian and they have Indian names.

I took it in stride until Sunday declared himself a fashion stylist. He began pointing out beautiful Nigerian women and suggested I pay attention. He urged me to invest in lipstick and high heels. As I sat in the car dressed like a hobo, I grew annoyed. How dare Sunday give me the exact same advice my parents and husband have given me for years?

My parents are stuck with me, and I have borne John three beloved children. Their criticism is blunted by love. Sunday was an independent observer who studied me in the rearview mirror, like fungus in a petri dish. His words stung.

I complained to my husband. My husband ignored me.

Then an okada clipped the car in a traffic jam. Sunday removed the key and attempted to chase down the driver, leaving John alone in a sweltering vehicle for twenty minutes while the police screamed at him and tried to extort money.

John feared Sunday would place his wife and children in a similarly volatile situation.

My husband had a talk with Sunday. John told him to improve or we would fire him.

After that conversation, Sunday stopped offering me pointers.

When Sunday reversed into the gutter by accident, I had to wade through green sludge to exit our SUV but I didn't mind. I knew it was only a matter of time before we hired a new driver.

*

The family settled deeper into Nigerian life. We enrolled the children at a new school. We left corporate housing and moved to a little house, around the corner from school. We were no longer daily hostages of the go-slow. Sunday stayed quiet. I began relaxing in the car.

Then one day, Sunday mentioned that he had a son who was late.

"Late for what?" I asked.

"He is no more," he said.

"No more what?" I asked.

"He died, Madame."

Oh. Oh, no. As my heart broke for Sunday's loss, deep down inside, the ugliest part of me said, "*Damn it!*"

After I learned that Sunday's son passed away in 2006, I told my husband we couldn't fire our driver just for being a terrible driver.

Sunday's son is *late*, I explained,and it would be cruel to add to his pain. Now we are stuck with Sunday until he kills us in a car wreck.

*

When we first met Sunday, we assumed he was elderly based on his baldness and wrinkled, shrunken appearance. His shoulders slumped. He wore his pants well above his natural waistline. He spent a large percentage of time napping in the car. John and I felt magnanimous for giving an employment opportunity to such an unqualified senior citizen.

One day, I asked Sunday if he fought in the Biafran War, which took place in the late '60s. Luckily he didn't understand my accent.

Guess what? I saw Sunday's drivers' license. He was born in 1969. He is forty-four years old, only a few years older than me.

In February, I asked him when his birthday was and, when he answered, I blinked.

"That's tomorrow," I said.

"Yes, Madame."

"Do you have plans?" I asked.

Sunday laughed. "I am a poor man, Madame."

"Well, is your wife going to make you a special meal at least?"

"Everything comes from my sweat. If I give her money to buy me a meal, she will make it. But I am poor, Madame."

Late Son + Poverty = Drive me to The Palms Mall so I can buy you a gift.

I gave Sunday a digital camera for his birthday.

He unpeeled the wrapping paper slowly. He stared at the box with wide eyes, his lips peeled back in fright. I couldn't understand his reaction. He behaved as if he'd been handed a bomb.

In the U.S., I had no household help. As a result, I don't know how to treat my staff in Nigeria. I do what feels natural and it's never correct.

Sunday had complimented my camera once so I thought he would like one of his own. Then John pointed out that he has no computer so it's useless to him.

It was so much less complicated in America, when I handled the housework by myself, when I drove around town in a filthy blue minivan.

*

Sunday has started asking for extras on top of his salary. Last month he requested a large sum of money to buy his children a TV. He said he wanted something simple and not a "lasma," which in Sunday's language means plasma.

72

We gave him the money. It's obvious that Sunday is trying.

After some lessons from John, Sunday has begun using his mirrors and glancing behind him before putting the car in reverse. He is determined to stop crashing.

Since he lacks innate driving ability, Sunday has developed a new technique to avoid accidents. He has begun driving slower than anyone else on the road including wandering goats.

The car dips in and out of a lone pothole as galaxies are born and die.

*

As an additional courtesy, Sunday no longer talks nonstop. He has a deep-seated need to express himself, however. We can see how much it pains him to remain quiet.

Now he *mutters*.

Sunday mutters all the time. It is maddening. Half of me wishes he would stop and half of me is dying to know what he's saying. Sunday mutters when other drivers yell at him for his low speeds. He mutters when collectors at the tollbooth yell at him for using the wrong lane. And he mutters when the police officers yell at him for trying to make illegal left turns.

But until the day we went to Ghana, I had never known what Sunday was muttering.

Let's start at the beginning. John and I woke up at 4:00 a.m. to finish packing before our flight. I got the kids dressed and gave them breakfast. We were all ready to go by 5:15, but where was Sunday? John called him. Sunday said he would be there soon.

He arrived an hour later.

When we finally climbed into the car at 6:20, John was furious. "Our flight is at 7:05. You were supposed to be here sixty-five minutes ago. If we miss our flight—and we will miss it—I am holding you responsible. I need a driver who's punctual."

For once, Sunday drove fast. John urged him to drive faster. And when he began muttering, I was sitting right behind him. I pushed my face against the headrest so I could catch what he was saying.

Sunday was mumbling, "JesuChristJesuChristJesuChrist-JesuChristOhLordJesuChristJesuChrist."

Mystery solved.

*

One day, I saw a woman slap her housemaid outside of Domino's Pizza. That night I dreamt I gave Sunday a vigorous beating. I boxed his ears until they bled.

I understand why my driver has seeped into my subconscious. As we approach the second anniversary of our move to Nigeria, being driven by Sunday remains a maddening experience.

When Sunday's malaria flared up last week, a company driver replaced him. The replacement was young, alert, a dynamo. He sped down side streets to avoid traffic jams. He plowed through potholes. He possessed a breathtaking mixture of intelligence and confidence. I arrived at Shoprite twenty minutes before I expected to.

We should have been *delighted*. Instead, John and I were relieved when Sunday returned. The replacement's competence terrified us. What if he used his cleverness to steal fuel money or kidnap our children?

We have grown accustomed to Sunday's plodding but honest demeanor. We trust him. We see how challenging Sunday finds driving a car. He has no spare mental energy to scheme.

*

Ultimately, does it matter if our driver can't drive well? Does it matter that we're often lost and never arrive anywhere on time?

No. We have decided to throw in our lot with Sunday.

As I fumble toward becoming a Nigerian Madame, I take my cues from my driver. I can tell he approves when I walk the children to their classrooms in the morning. He likes when I wear Ankara dresses and wear my hair loose down my back. He roars with laughter when we try to speak Pidgin.

Sunday scowls if I come back from a party and I've had too much to drink. And whenever I have lunch with a male friend, Sunday looks murderous. The only men who meet his approval are himself and his Oga, my husband.

He drives around town at a snail's pace, but so what? There are worse things.

We crept past a four car-pileup on Awolowo Road just this morning, Sunday muttering something I didn't quite catch. A reckless driver in Lagos would be disastrous.

*

In my previous incarnation as a New Jersey housewife, I had intended to trade in my minivan for something sporty like a Mini when the kids grew up. I never imagined I'd live out my days in Nigeria, relying on Sunday to drive me around.

But life moves in surprising directions that can't be plotted in advance. It meanders like a mumbling Igbo driver inching down a bumpy road. Though frustrating, the journey has grown richer for all the twists and turns.

MOBILE HOMELESS

James Stark

A January cold front out of the Gulf of Alaska brought damp frosty air and intermittent snow flurries into the city and our neighborhood. I wondered whether the rust bucket on wheels, aka the Volkswagen van parked in front of my house for the last several days, might be harboring someone who was in danger of freezing. Indeed, the van had become a talking point on our block, where neighbors, although friendly, otherwise keep to themselves.

"Do you have a child home from school?" Agnes, a widow and retired teacher from across the street, wanted to know.

"No, I don't," I replied. I didn't need to ask why she wanted to know.

"Well, it's that…that thing parked in front of your house. To whom do you suppose it belongs?"

"Not a clue," I answered. "But I'll look into it," I promised.

It's usually quiet on Fairview Lane and the lawns are garnished in season with borders of flowers, tastefully arranged. The hedges of red-tip photinia, laurel and boxwood are neatly trimmed and never encroach over daily swept sidewalks. The houses on our street are not elegant, but they are painted and roofed before there is evidence of need. Some houses even boast solar panels on roof tops, despite our usually gray and overcast Seattle skies.

The sixties era van had four bald tires and a treadless spare mounted on its front. Stickers with slogans protesting various shortcomings of society or the malfeasance of various municipal, state, and federal governments conveniently masked the van's rusting metal. The out of state license plates were current.

Curtains covered most of the windows, obscuring whatever life might reside within.

On our street we aren't used to irregularities. Neighbors know and greet each other as they walk to the nearby bus stop or climb into their hybrid cars on their way to work. A few hardy souls don bicycle helmets and roll up cuffs as they pedal into the morning traffic. So when neighbor Agnes expressed her concern about the VW I was "hosting," it fell to me to take action before other neighbors checked in. Besides, I was concerned about leaving my house for a planned trip to the sun of Hawaii while an uninvited guest posed a potential problem in front of it.

As I planned my course of action from my living room, the van's age drew me back to an experience I had in my own youth. In college, my first love was a bright young woman from a well-to-do family. We had made plans and swore undying love, between exams and term papers. Before a particularly difficult chemistry final (we were both in pre-med), she decided to answer the lure of long distance and left me and college to follow the open-ended promise of the road "before she got bogged down in the life that was planned for her." She was 'California Dreamin,' as she put it, and threw a backpack into an earlier version of this same VW van and climbed in next to a man I didn't know, who wore a beard I couldn't have grown, with a tie-dyed shirt, love beads, and sandals I would never have worn. She drove out of my life and never looked back.

Nostalgia or not, I had promised Agnes I would look into the van. I called around on both sides of the block. How embarrassing, I thought, to have a neighbor's friend's car towed? No college-aged kids or friends laid claim to the vehicle. Indeed, no one had seen a VW of that vintage since they were in college themselves. Some of my neighbors even speculated humorously that I was trying to relive my own youth.

When my daily paper went missing from the porch, the level of seriousness became heightened. I printed out a sign and placed it on the van's windshield. "Is this an abandoned vehicle?" the sign asked, without greeting or signature. What was I expecting, I wondered? A polite, hand-written note to the effect that "No, I certainly wouldn't abandon my only means of transportation and shelter in the coldest part of the year. I'm living here now. Drop by for tea sometime."

After several calls to city departments, I learned there is no law against sleeping in a car in the city of Seattle up to seventy-two hours. And, further, that it would take at least fourteen days for a traffic official to determine whether the van was, in fact, abandoned. Those are 'working days,' no weekends, holidays, and not counting furlough days for city employees in the current economic recession. There would be another seventy-two hours before a warning was posted on the vehicle and a tow truck was called. And, finally, the tow company had fourteen days in which to remove the interloper from the street.

Even though there was no quick fix here, I decided to take the next step, even if it required my version of street theater to mobilize the creaky mechanisms of government. With the first call to the city, I identified myself and provided my address. With the subsequent calls, I disguised my voice, alternating a high-pitched voice with a deep basso. With each call I emphasized my fear of potential crime activity. I enjoy movies whose characters have accents. And I particularly like the Slavic accents. They seem to drop the articles and invert the word order: "Is van park-ed in street too long time," I say in my best imitation of the Ukrainian who painted my house last year. Then I attempted the accents of the Mexicans, or were they Nicaraguans, who roofed my house several years ago.

"There ees a folks wag`on in frente of thee house. Ju want thee number of thee car and thee house?"

Clearly, these calls were not working to move the wheels of bureaucracy any faster than the old VW's ascent up a steep Seattle hill.

The first time I saw a light inside the van, I was emboldened to attempt the direct approach. No threats, just an offer of gas money to move on; park in some other neighborhood. At least he'd know he wasn't anonymous; that people were aware and watching.

"Is there somebody home in there?" I asked finally, one overcast, rainy morning, as I tapped on the driver's side window with my class ring, the only ring I had left on any finger since my divorce some years ago. The accent was mine: Northwest US, where we say "warsh" for wash or 'Warshington'. After my third knock on the window, a hand appeared, tentatively, to move an improvised curtain, followed by a head, wearing a wool Andean-style cap with ear flaps, over a clean-shaven, rather intelligent-looking face of a forty-ish man. Through the dirty windows, I made out cords and wires and parts of computers. He was not the picture of down-and-out I had imagined, which came with a beard, long hair, dirty and possibly smelly clothes. This was not a typical street bum with a vehicle, or, like my father used to call them, a "knight of the open road."

The local and national media carried on non-stop about the plight of the unemployed and homeless in America. I always assumed addiction and mental health problems were the cause. There was TV coverage of the tent cities like the Hoovervilles during the Great Depression. But this was my first sighting of a homeless man living in his vehicle, in my neighborhood, right in front of my house.

"Are you all right in there," I asked, at first feigning concern.

"Uh, yes, "he said. "Thanks for asking. Thanks for your concern."

"Do you need anything?" I asked, more worried that he would pee on my prize rose beds. Or worse. I recalled hearing on a news segment that any one of us could be in similar straits after missing a few months' paychecks. You can only live on credit cards for so long. The utilities get turned off; the rent payments pile up, as do the eviction notices. Not to mention the mortgage foreclosures. But what concerned me and my neighbors was that desperate people in those circumstances might resort to illegal activities. Certainly, 'not in our backyard.' We all do pay our taxes. After all, property values are at risk.

Isn't there some agency that provides for these people? Where do they go to carry on their business, their human necessities; dump their trash, I wondered to myself?

"No. No thank you," the man in the window replied politely in a soft voice. "I'm sorry for the inconvenience. Things have gotten difficult. I lost my job. My wife…she moved in with her parents, took the kids…"

He was embarrassed. Or at least, I thought he should be. I would be. But I'm not in his situation; and after my plans to offer him money for gas and maybe expenses to move on stuck in my throat, I didn't know what to do. "I'm sorry," I said, "Times are hard."

I retreated to my porch. From there I could see my neighbor, Agnes, watching the goings-on across the street. We both observed him through our curtained windows, our eyes meeting briefly, as he pushed his own wrinkled and dirty curtain back across the window and opened the van's door. He climbed out, closed the door, locked it, and walked hurriedly across the street and down the block without looking back. And that was the last I saw of him.

Some days later, I saw the notice on his windshield announcing that the impound date for the vehicle's removal. There would, of course, be towing charges, as well as daily storage fees until the vehicle was claimed. At last, I thought, I could almost hear the corroded gears of our municipal bureaucracy engaging and starting to move. I got out of bed earlier than usual on the 18th of February, the day before the impound, and drew aside the curtains. The van was gone. I rushed out to the sidewalk to confirm that the old clunker hadn't been moved farther down the block. Seeing nothing, I celebrated my righteous victory of order over chaos with a fist pump.

But, like a sneaker wave at the ocean, an unfamiliar emotion caught me off guard. What would the guy do now, I asked myself? Was this remorse I felt? Regret? Or was it, so help me, payback on my part for my own personal loss of a girlfriend to a similar vehicle so many decades ago? But the man in front of my house had nothing really to do with my love lost to a vagabond in another VW van so long ago. I shrugged away those bygone images and the pain they had caused, as I dismissed any thoughts about the owner of the current van and his loss of safe place to park. I walked back onto my porch, retrieved my morning paper, and moved toward the warmth of my orderly kitchen and the smell of freshly brewed coffee.

TO THE PASSENGER IN SEAT C

dl mattila

I wonder why you're so inclined
with each explosive exhalation,
to bless my soul each time I sneeze;
renounce this social obligation.

The origin of your response
is wrapped in lore of evil spirit;
resist the urge—but if you must—
consider words of greater merit.

In your attempt to wish me well
when plague and demon beg evicting,
in lieu of *Proost, Salud, God Bless*,
I might prefer *You're so good looking*.

CURIOUS IN CORSICA:
A TALE OF TWO COUPLES

Mary Donaldson-Evans

"Go ahead. Say something interesting, Louis. I dare you."

The female voice, heard above the buzz of a fish tank, came from a neighboring table in the dining room of La Dolce Vita, a Corsican hotel where my husband and I were spending the last days of a Mediterranean vacation. We exchanged a glance. Having seen the couple twice a day for the past three days, I'd entertained the idea of asking them to join us at our table, since we, like them, were alone in Corsica.

"We could share travel stories," I'd suggested to my husband, Jeff. Who knows? Maybe, like us, they'd left kids back home in the care of grandparents.

Jeff was unconvinced, and we'd continued to converse quietly while we ate, just a few feet away from this couple with whom I imagined we had much in common.

Now I knew he'd been right to hesitate. Popping the last piece of my croissant into my mouth, I shifted in my seat so that I could observe the other couple discreetly. The woman was unsmiling, her manicured hands folding and unfolding a sheet of ragged blue paper that seemed to be a letter. The man, slightly balding and a little thick around the middle, looked at his wife—I assumed she was his wife; they were both wearing wedding rings—with concern. Did I imagine it, or had his eyes filled with tears when she delivered her cruel remark? In any case, he didn't take the bait. Perhaps he really didn't have anything interesting to say.

He glanced in my direction, and I lowered my eyes in time to see him stretch out his left leg towards hers.

She drew her foot back sharply.

My mind went into overdrive. What was with this couple? What could have prompted such a hostile remark? All couples said cutting things to each other now and then, even Jeff and I. But this was somehow beyond the pale. She was wrinkling her nose as if she could barely stand to breathe the same air as the man sitting opposite her. Why did he disgust her so? And then I knew; I just knew. She, a modern Emma Bovary, born to enjoy all of life's refinements, had tired of searching for her Prince and had settled for this dull specimen of masculinity. His hands were probably clammy, his handshake limp. Why had she married him? Was he wealthy? They were, after all, vacationing in Corsica. But then again, so were we, and we were solidly middle class. I glanced around the dining room, taking in the polished cotton tablecloths with huge sunflowers on a turquoise background, the red industrial carpeting, the crayfish crawling around the fish tank. No, if they'd been wealthy, they'd have booked in at a better hotel. There had to be another reason. He was a fireman, maybe, and he'd pulled her mother from a burning building. Or a lenient judge who had taken pity on her sister, a thieving heroin addict, and had sentenced her to a stint in rehab rather than to prison. He was clearly in love with his wife; you could see it in his eyes, in the way his body leaned towards hers.

So she'd said "I do," and the day after the wedding she'd awakened to find him next to her, snoring softly, his eyes puffy. "This is the man I've chosen to share my life with," she thought, and a feeling of revulsion overcame her.

Satisfied that I'd solved the mystery of their relationship, I tapped my husband on the arm and we left the dining room. I felt sorry for this unhappy couple, sorrier for him than for her. He didn't deserve to be treated with such scorn. I thought about them all morning as we toured the port of Bonifacio with its limestone cliffs, continued to think about them as we drove alongside the thickly forested hills known as the maquis, where bandits were reputed to have hidden as recently as the nineteenth century. I was still thinking about them as we lunched on cannelloni filled with bruccio, a fragrant local goat cheese.

And then, as we were returning to the hotel, I spotted a wad of crumpled blue paper in a flower pot by the entrance. The letter! Who had discarded it here, and why? I was mystified. Then that demon curiosity got the better of me. Glancing around to make sure nobody was looking, I slid it into my pocket. Back in the room, I spread it out on the table and started to read.

My Dearest Louis,

Be patient, my love. In just ten more days, you'll be rid of that insufferable bitch and we can begin our life together. I can't stand to be without you. You are so handsome, so sexy, easily the most interesting man I've ever known.

I gasped. Louis was a philanderer! He deserved to be insulted. His wife was the wronged party, not him. I tried to wrap my mind around the idea of this non-descript middle-aged man cheating on his wife. It wasn't easy. Then I read on. The letter, saturated with all the platitudes of romantic love—sunsets, dinners by candlelight, wine, roses—was signed "Barbara," and whoever "Barbara" was, she'd clearly been involved with Louis for some time. She was glad "that Jag of yours can't talk" ("Good God," I thought, "what were they, teenagers?") and she wrote with shocking clarity about certain parts of Louis's body that she found irresistible. I gulped, strangely aroused by the letter's graphic details, despite the fact that the description was completely at odds with the impression I'd formed of Louis. I turned to look at the lean, toned body of my husband who was lying on the bed, reading a guidebook.

"I'm going to take a shower, honey." I pulled my T-shirt over my head. "Care to join me?"

Two hours later, as we headed down to the dining room

for dinner, we crossed Louis's wife on the stairs. She had dark glasses on, so I couldn't see if she'd been crying.

"Probably forgot something in the room," I thought. "Meds, maybe. With what she's going through, she has to be on Valium."

Curiously, though, she didn't come back down, and Louis dined by himself at his usual table. He was wearing espadrilles with an open-necked shirt and white linen pants. He looked more respectable than he had at breakfast time. Less flabby, for one thing, and almost European. The top three buttons of his navy blue silk shirt had been left unbuttoned, revealing a curl of graying chest hair.

We'd just ordered an appetizer of fish bisque with crostini when the waiter brought Louis his main course. He'd chosen the veal stuffed with spinach and goat cheese rather than the monkfish.

"I'll have the monkfish," said Jeff when the waiter asked for our main course selection. He was always watching his weight, that husband of mine, always mindful of his cholesterol and his blood pressure, always going for the healthy choice. Furthermore, he never, ever ate veal or foie gras. It was the animal cruelty thing. He knew too much about how food got from the farm to the table, and he was appalled by what he'd read about the treatment of calves and geese.

"I'll take the veal," I said, glancing over at Louis's plate.

Jeff gave me a disapproving look.

"What?!" I asked, defiant.

He said nothing.

I looked back at Louis and tried to catch his eye, but he was too busy tucking into his veal. I was a little scandalized that he seemed to be enjoying his dinner so much. I imagined his wife upstairs in their room, sprawled across the bed, crying her eyes out. What would she do for dinner? This little hotel had no room service. Would Louis ask if, exceptionally, they could send up a tray? The least he could do would be to wrap up a bread roll and take it to her.

"I was thinking that we might want to visit Napoleon Bonaparte's boyhood home tomorrow," said Jeff. "It's in Ajaccio."

"Sure, honey, that'd be great," I said, noticing that the waiter was refilling Louis's wine glass for the third time.

I didn't get to find out if Louis was going to sneak bread up to his wife, because he was still at the table when we left the dining room, lingering over what remained of his bottle of wine. His cheeks were a bit flushed now, his eyes slightly glazed. It could be my imagination, but he just didn't seem all that remorseful. He even gave me an appreciative glance as we brushed past his table. "I'm probably more his type than his wife," I thought. "Maybe I even remind him of Barbara."

I noticed for the first time that he had nice eyes.

We slept in the next morning and almost missed breakfast. Jeff didn't seem to mind. "How about a little roll in the hay?" he teased, pulling me towards him.

"I'd rather have a roll with butter and jam," I countered. "I'm hungry!"

"So am I," he winked.

But there would be time later to satisfy that kind of hunger. I leapt out of bed, pulled on my blue capri pants and a white T-shirt, and ran a comb through my short brown hair.

"Hurry! We'll be late!" I urged Jeff. He was a little grumpy now, but he obliged, sleepily dressing and heading for the door.

"Wait!" I said, as he reached for the room keys.

He was wearing dress socks with sandals.

It took him only a minute to change—I had to confess that he was a good sport—and within five minutes we were seated at our table in the dining room.

They were there. Both of them.

This time I focused on her. She was certainly put together;

you had to give her that. Her long, honey-brown hair was streaked with blond, the kind of streaking that can only be produced by chemicals and foil and endless hours at the beauty salon. Her make-up was impeccable. Her eyelashes were too thick to be her own, however, and her straight nose was just slightly off-center, a dead giveaway. This was a woman who worshipped at the altar of Aphrodite, who'd been willing to sign pre-surgical waivers warning her that what she was about to do might result in disfigurement or even death, in order to achieve her ideal of physical perfection. This was a woman who'd chosen a lipstick color to match the varnish on her fingers and toes.

She wore a soft yellow tank top, a floral-print cotton miniskirt, and strappy sandals. Her legs were long and shapely, the kind of legs you see on models in glossy magazines, the kind of legs real women almost never have.

I felt a little less sorry for her. Maybe she was an "insufferable bitch." Maybe she was a cold fish, more concerned with keeping her make-up from smudging than with pleasing her husband. Maybe she'd driven Louis into the arms of the other woman.

I took a sip of coffee and turned my attention to Louis. He was eating bread and jam and reading a copy of the local newspaper, *Corse Matin*. But wait! That meant he must know French! Was he French? Corsican? I suddenly realized that in the few snippets of conversation we'd heard, she was the one who'd been doing the talking. We hadn't actually heard him say more than a word or two, too little to detect a foreign accent. But if he could read a newspaper in French with such apparent absorption, he must know the language. Maybe his name was pronounced "loo-ee" and not "lew-is." That hadn't been part of my scenario.

Suddenly he looked up from his newspaper and met my eyes. I actually blushed. Blushed! Where had I read that people over forty no longer blushed, that it was physiologically impossible?

But there was no mistaking that hot, flushed feeling that crept into my face. Embarrassed, I downed the last dregs of my café au lait and we headed out to do our day's sightseeing.

Ajaccio was on the itinerary for today, our second-to-last day in Corsica. As we made our way through the clogged streets in our bright green Peugeot, I looked in vain for the couple from the hotel restaurant. Perhaps they were back at the hotel, sorting out their problems. Or maybe they'd decided to head out to the country, where pigs ambled alongside the road and the free-roaming goats nibbled on the pungent vegetation that flourishes on the island and gives it its seductive aroma. Whatever the case, they certainly weren't missing much in Ajaccio. With the exception of one room on the first floor, Napoleon's childhood home was all but stripped of its furniture, and I couldn't work up much enthusiasm for the documents and other artifacts displayed in cases around the rooms. I mean, I was supposed to get excited about Bonaparte's mother's leather glove? Really, now! As for the Musée Fesch, our next stop, it certainly failed to live up to its description in the Michelin Guide. Unless you happen to be passionate about Madonna and child paintings, which were here in abundance, there wasn't much to see, and the great Renaissance artists— Titian, Botticelli, Veronese, etc.—were represented by about one canvas each, while most of the walls were covered with paintings by artists we'd never heard of. Even Jeff, who has a special fondness for the Renaissance and is way more cultured than I am, conceded that the museum was disappointing. As we were leaving, one of the portraits did attract my attention, though. It was one of those paintings in which the subject's eyes seem to follow you wherever you go. I stopped and looked more closely. They were Louis's eyes!

Back at the hotel, we were beginning to climb the steps to our room when I heard a male voice behind me, at the reception desk:

"Nous partons demain. Pourriez-vous préparer la note, s'il vous plaît?"

It was Louis! So he was French! His voice was deeper than I imagined it to be.

At dinner, I noticed for the first time that he held his cutlery in the European way, the fork prongs down, the knife never leaving his left hand. His wife, apparently lost in thought, didn't even spare him a glance, and he appeared indifferent to her now too. They exchanged no words. I wondered how long it'd be before the divorce papers were filed. Would Barbara be waiting for him when he returned home?

His wife finished her meal quickly and got up from the table, leaving Louis to his bottle of red wine. Jeff and I drank wine by the glass, and my glass was empty. I summoned the waiter and asked for another. Then, raising it to my lips, I looked back at Louis. He met my gaze and—was it possible?— he gave me a "come hither" look. I was mortified. I wasn't that kind of a woman! Turning to face my husband, I grabbed his hand and squeezed it. There! That would show him!

But apparently it didn't, because on his way out of the dining room, Louis stopped at our table and introduced himself, first giving my husband a firm handshake, European-style (no pumping, just one vigorous downward thrust), then turning to me, taking my hand in his and raising my fingers to his lips. His hands were dry and warm. And when he leaned over me and said, "Enchanté, Madame," I got a whiff of his cologne, some spicy French scent, I think. It was only after he'd left that I noticed he'd dropped a scrap of paper in my lap. On it was written, in that script that is so easily recognizable as European: "Chambre N°16, 11h."

What?! He expected me to go to his room? Their room? Did he envision a threesome? Or were they occupying separate rooms now? Either way, I flushed with rage and humiliation. The gall! Couldn't he see that I was wholesome and virtuous?

Couldn't he tell that I was happily married?

I passed the note to Jeff.

"Well, it's hardly surprising," he said, visibly titillated by the fact that another man had designs on me. "You haven't taken your eyes off him for the past three days."

"But I wasn't flirting," I protested.

"Well, no," he acknowledged. He had no reason to worry, and he knew it. "But this is Europe. A stare means something here."

He leaned across the table and kissed me gently. And then he, too, broke our iron-clad rule by ordering a second glass of wine.

It was a balmy night. The high winds of the previous day had calmed, and when we returned to our room, we threw open the windows to the sea and drank in the fragrant night air.

"A little warm in here, don't you think?" asked Jeff, slipping my gauzy dress over my shoulders.

I closed my eyes and made love with Louis that night, without once betraying Jeff. Riding the waves of my fantasy, I felt the heat of a throbbing passion I hadn't known since the early days of my twenty year-old marriage. We fell asleep in each other's arms.

When I awoke the next morning, I turned to look at Jeff, admiring his full head of blond hair, his strong chin. He had a nerdy side—he was a college professor after all—but beneath the horn-rimmed glasses and the button-down shirts, he was pretty sexy. Sensing my gaze, he opened his eyes, smiled, and tousled my hair.

"Welcome back," he laughed.

SOMEWHERE IN THE HEART OF ROME

Robert Sachs

The taxi stops on the Via della Stamperia near the Trevi Fountain, the driver raising his hands in frustration. "That way. That," he says, grappling for the few English words he knows and pointing to a narrow street on the other side of the fountain he can't reach. Herman Cogan understands. He pays the driver and, picking up his suitcase, sets off toward the hotel he hopes he will find not too far down that narrow street. He stops first at the famous Trevi Fountain. How could he not? He has seen the movie and wonders now if he, too, can find romance in Rome. He puts his suitcase down, takes one of the Italian coins the taxi driver had given him in change, and tosses it in the water. "Make it mine," he whispers before moving on.

Cogan will be in Rome for one week, courtesy of the insurance company he has represented for twelve years. This is the benefit bestowed for being one of its best producers. He sees his life as modest and mundane, but this suits him. He sells debit life insurance to people in his Chicago neighborhood. He attends Shabbat morning services regularly at the synagogue not three blocks from his apartment. But, for Cogan, this is a day of firsts: the first time in his forty years he's ventured outside the United States. Even during the war, he was stationed at Fort Bragg, but never saw action. It's his first time on a jet plane, the first time he has to deal with foreign currency and, of course, his first time in Rome. He's exhausted and in need of sleep, but he is also excited at being in the City of the Seven Hills.

The summer sun overwhelms the off-white walls of his hotel room, making them sparkle when what he craves, in his exhaustion, is darkness. From his vantage point at the window of this third floor room, with his hand on the drape cord, he sees, lying on her back, at the edge of the hotel pool below, a young woman wearing only the bottom half of her bikini. Cogan never thought of himself as a voyeur, but maybe, he realizes now, that was because the opportunity hadn't presented itself. He stands there, dog-tired and totally transfixed.

The woman, motionless, with close-cropped dark brown hair, is shapely and long. On her right breast is a small tattoo of a five-pointed star. Her thin left ankle is crossed over her right and, around it, is a gold bracelet. He wonders if this means she is left-handed, and then he laughs at himself for noticing her ankle bracelet when there are so many more important parts of her to appreciate. As he stares, he thinks he sees a blink behind the woman's gray sunglasses. *Has she spotted me?* He hurriedly closes the drapes and backs away from the window.

He sighs as he lowers himself to the bed. There he lies for a minute, maybe two, thinking of the beautiful woman sunning herself below his window. What a country, he says. He wonders if this is normal for women in Italy. Or is she a harlot? When he is no longer able to contain himself, he goes again to the window. The woman is on her stomach now, stretched out on a yellow beach towel, reading a book. Her back is beautifully tanned and Cogan imagines her spine as a riverbed leading to a tiny pool just above her round, white, bikinied buttocks. She raises her head and peaks over her glasses at a waiter who leans down to hand her a note. She opens it and turns to look up. Cogan is sure this time that she is looking directly at him and he moves quickly from the window, letting the drape fall back into place.

At five-thirty, he checks the window again—the woman is gone. A fat, balding man, smoking a cigar and wearing a black and white flowered bikini brief swimsuit covered in front almost entirely by the overhang of his belly, is sitting on a hardwood chaise, reading a newspaper. Cogan dresses and goes downstairs. The travel package includes dinners at the hotel restaurant, which is directly across the lobby from the front desk. But when he tries the door, it's locked. At the desk, the clerk tells him dinner service will begin at eight.

"It is our custom," he says in response to the quizzical look on Cogan's face.

More firsts, he thinks: naked women, fat men in tiny swimsuits, dinner close to bedtime. Cogan marvels at the peculiar customs he's been exposed to in such a brief time. *What next?* he wonders.

Armed with a map provided by the hotel, he finds his way to the Colosseum. The late afternoon sun is hot and the walk has made him sweaty. He marvels at the structure while looking for an entrance that would get him inside. When he sees the ticket office is closed for the day, he moves on to a small street that gently rises above the heavily trafficked Via Celio Vibenna. Here he sits in the shade of a stone pine tree with an unobstructed view of the iconic circular monument. The magnificent view, a cool breeze, and the steady hum of traffic below him add to his fatigue, and he is soon asleep.

It is almost eight when he awakens. Seeing the Colosseum and the lights of the city makes him smile. Walking back to the hotel in the dusk, Cogan loses his way and finds himself on the Via Sacra in the middle of the famous Roman Forum. He spots the Arch of Titus. Finding it on his map puts him back on course and, as he passes through the Arch, he sees a young woman passionately kissing an older, well-dressed man. The *City of Love*, he thinks.

Cogan gets back to the hotel after nine. The door to the restaurant is now open and almost every table is taken. The maître d' asks if he'd mind sharing a table with another guest. Cogan says not at all. He realizes that in Chicago he would have said no and waited for a solo table. Whether the difference is being in Rome or just being so far from home, Cogan isn't sure, but he senses adventure and, to his surprise, it doesn't frighten him. He is seated at a table for two with a plump woman he gauges to be about his age.

"Good evening. Herman Cogan. Chicago, Illinois."

"Hi. Rhoda Finkelstein. New York. It looks like the Fates have thrown us together."

"Vacationing?" he asks, pleased with his newfound boldness. The woman has a pleasant smile and, when she puts her napkin to her mouth, he sees she is not wearing a wedding ring. Thoughts skim through Cogan's brain faster than he can process.

"No, actually. I'm here on business," she says. I'm a buyer for Saks."

He must not have heard right. "You buy sacks?"

Rhoda Finkelstein laughs. "Could be. If they're fashionable enough. Saks Fifth Avenue."

"Ah," he says.

During dinner, he finds out she was born in Brooklyn and, until she got the job at Saks, traveled very little. She talks freely about herself and listens attentively when Cogan speaks. He notices a small tattoo on the inside of her left wrist, half hidden by her wristwatch. It looks like the same five-pointed star he saw on the breast of the woman at the pool. "I like your tattoo," he says. "Does it mean anything?"

"Thanks. Just a design I like."

"I think I've seen one like it before."

"They're popular," she says. "It's called the nautical star."

They both order the same dessert: chocolate gelato. When they finish, Rhoda stands and holds out her hand. "Nice to meet you, Herman" she says. "I have to look for a friend. I sent her a note about dinner, but she seems to have misunderstood." They shake hands and she disappears into the hotel lobby. Cogan sits for a while, drinking the last of a warm glass of water, thinking about Rhoda Finkelstein. Very attractive, very pleasant. He notices a tall, attractive woman with close-cropped dark hair standing at the door to the restaurant, leaning in on tiptoes, as if looking for someone. He must have been staring without being conscious of it, because the woman smiles and lowers her eyes. Embarrassed, Cogan looks away, but he realizes it is the woman from the pool. How odd, he thinks, to be looking at a fully clothed stranger knowing that, a few hours earlier, he had seen her—what was the term his friend Stern used—precious assets. He watches as she walks back through the lobby to the elevator. Cogan thinks she is as lovely with clothes as she was earlier without. He fantasizes bringing such a woman back to Chicago, introducing her at his synagogue. The imagined reactions of his fellow congregants make him smile. He isn't generally known as a lady's man and he thinks of himself as being painfully shy around women. After a few minutes, he leaves the restaurant and goes to his room, hoping to quickly fall asleep.

Next morning, he is sitting on a bench in front of a small bookstore close to the hotel, thumbing through a guidebook to Rome, when he sees Rhoda and the woman with the anklet leave the hotel. Cogan is amazed the two women know one another. He decides to follow them, although he's not sure why. It dawns on him as he trails behind at a safe distance that the anklet woman could be a model working with Rhoda to help her select merchandise. The women are headed toward the Roman Forum. With fewer people on the street now, Cogan drops farther back. He catches a glimpse of them near the Arch of Titus. In the darkness of its shadow, he sees the anklet woman pull Rhoda to her; they kiss in a quick embrace and then walk on, now holding hands. *What is it about this arch?* he wonders.

While he is not worldly, Cogan, nonetheless, is aware that there are women attracted to other women. These are the first he's ever met, however, and he would never have guessed. Not that he's actually met the anklet woman, but he has seen a lot of her. Cogan thinks both, in their own ways, are feminine and certainly attractive to men—at least they're attractive to him. He wonders what brought them together. While he feels some disappointment that he will not find romance with either of them, he feels relieved as well. Relieved, because his few forays into relationships with the opposite sex have been stressful affairs. Perhaps, he thinks, this opens the door to a more relaxed liaison with the women, a simple friendship.

That evening as he enters the hotel restaurant, Rhoda waves at him. "Over here, Herman." She's sitting with the anklet woman near the rear of the restaurant. "Herman, this is Fina. Fina, Herman. We were just talking about you."

He shakes hands with both of them and sits down. Cogan finds Fina charming. She speaks excellent English with a soft Italian accent. The women tell him of their visit to the Vatican. He tells them of his tour of the Great Synagogue of Rome and his walk through the Jewish ghetto.

"So we've got the religious part covered," laughs Rhoda.

"And how do you two know each other?" he asks.

The women look at one another. Rhoda answers: "We met some years ago on one of my buying trips. Fina was modeling at the time. We've remained friends ever since."

"Good friends," Fina adds. Cogan smiles. He wonders if there will ever be a time when he can tell Fina he saw her sunbathing, or if she already knows. His face reddens at the thought.

When Rhoda invites him to join them on a boat tour along the Tiber in the morning he says, "Why not?"

At one point on the boat, Fina notices Cogan looking at a young woman in high heels and shorts lean over the starboard rail. "You like women, eh, Herman?" He's not offended by the question. He remembers in high school, when the cute girl sitting in the next row asked him to look at his fingernails. He bent his fingers toward his palm and, looking, asked, "What's wrong with my nails?"

The girl giggled. "If you did this," she said holding her fingers straight with the back of her hand facing her, "you'd be a homo." He laughed then, pleased that he'd passed the test, but he wondered what it was about him that led her to ask the question in the first place. Did he seem gay? Had she asked other guys? Fina's question was similar, but more in the nature of whether he was a member of the club.

He smiles. "Yes, women, of course."

"Fina was born here," Rhoda interrupts. "She can show us all the best places. Stick with us, Herman. Better than roaming the streets alone."

"Yes, yes," Fina says, "Please, Herman."

It was an odd invitation from women who kiss and hold hands. But Cogan thinks he knows why he is being invited: They've made a calculation that he's harmless. And, perhaps, being with him will keep other admirers at bay. With a touch of sadness, he concludes they are right. "I'd love to," he says.

Fina moves next to him and makes a show of kissing him on the cheek. "Hold it," Rhoda says, taking aim with her camera. "I'll send you prints, Herman."

Harmless, he thinks, and maybe charming.

Both women are wide-eyed at everything they see. "Herman, look. Look!" Rhoda yells. He smiles and is amazed at the enthusiasm he didn't expect from this sophisticated New Yorker. Yet Rhoda seems to approach everything with gusto. Fina, too, a native of Rome, overflows with excitement. In this regard, they seem to Cogan like grownup children.

And so goes Cogan's remaining days in Rome. He squires Rhoda and Fina around the city—the ruins, the churches, the squares, the wonderful out-of-the-way bistros—all the while with one or the other of them by his side, holding his hand, squeezing his shoulder, kissing his cheek. He wants to tell them that it's okay for them to hold hands and kiss one another, that he knows and understands. But he says nothing.

On the day before he is to leave, the three of them are alone by the hotel pool, Fina in her bikini, Rhoda in a man's stripped shirt and pedal pushers, and Cogan in tan slacks and a pullover. The women are in high spirits.

Rhoda hands her camera to Cogan and sits on the hardwood chaise next to Fina. "Take our picture," she says.

"Wait," Fina says, as she casually and, with no outward appearance of shame, takes off her bikini top. "Now." Cogan's hands are shaking and he wonders if he'll be able to hold still long enough to get a clear photo. He imagines people are looking down at them from their hotel room windows and he wonders what they must be thinking.

"Now you," Rhoda says. "Over here." She takes the camera from Cogan's hands and pushes him toward the chaise.

*

The morning of his departure, both women are in the lobby to see him off. Using Rhoda's camera, the man behind the desk takes a picture of the trio. Herman in the middle with his arms around both Rhoda and Fina. Both hug Cogan and kiss him on the cheek. His thoughts on the flight back are more about Fina and Rhoda than the Colosseum and the Palatine. Romance? No, not in the traditional sense. But a good time? Definitely yes. *They were fun*, he told himself. *I had a great time.* He was happy. The coin he threw in the Trevi Fountain worked. Not in the way he had hoped but, nonetheless, in a good way.

*

Two weeks after Cogan's return home, a brown envelope containing twenty photos arrives with a note from Rhoda (*If you ever get to New York*, etc.) and a card for 10% off his purchases at Saks Fifth Avenue.

"Did you meet anyone?" his friend, Stern, asks.

"Two lovely women."

"So tell me."

He brings out the photographs, but he holds back for now—probably forever—the one of Fina and him taken at the pool. "Rhoda and Fina," he says.

"Fina. Nice name. She's the tall one, yes?" Stern begins his questioning in earnest as he examines each photo. How did you meet them? Which one did you like the best? What did you do together? Did you invite them to Chicago? Are there plans to see them again? And on. Stern, whose drugstore Cogan visits at the end of each workday for an Alka-Seltzer and conversation, is not, in Cogan's experience, close-mouthed. He will tell customers about his, Cogan's, trip to Italy and most definitely about the two women he was with in Rome. The word will spread. Some people at the synagogue will kid him: "Cogan, two women!" Or, "Next time I'm going with you." Friends will ask to see the photographs.

Cogan knows he is bragging through Stern. He also knows, in leaving out a key fact about Rhoda and Fina, he is being dishonest. But, he reasons, he is helping the women. *Is that not a mitzvah?* With a name like Rhoda Finkelstein, someone here could know an aunt or a second cousin of Rhoda's. Is it not better to keep quiet about her relationship with Fina? And if someone looking at the photos should get the wrong idea about him and these two lovely women, well, he concludes, he can live with that.

SHOOING FLIES

David Havird

I found the car key.
Maybe I ought to have sped to the port.
Thanks to a taxi, you were there
even ahead of time awaiting the ferry.

Instead, I braved the switchbacks,
narrow, gear-strippingly steep,
up that treeless rock
whose peak is St. Simeon's perch.

I pictured you, umbrellaed, gazing the harbor.
Lean out from under the shade and shoot your gaze
up to the blue-domed church.
Is somebody up there waving?

I meant to distance myself
as far as I could from the port of return,
spirit from body. Away, though,
hadn't we relished our bodies!

Out in the bay where a fisherman
netted an icon depicting the Virgin,
beside her whitewashed church
on the severed tip of a finger of stone

I'd fished for you with my eyes,
then handled ashore love's shivering body,
which ached for another, the friction,
to redden its blue-lipped flame.

Who would have dreamed there'd be above it all
a nimbus of flies! Somebody, yes,
was waving and, bitten as if by sparks,
shooing flies.

A FAREWELL TO FARMS

Kevin Quigley

The *Limousin* landscape was as lush as I'd imagined. Even on a late-autumn evening, it felt like a midsummer day. Birdsong and the buzzing of dying bees filled the air. I was tired and sore, but even the sweat trapped under my backpack failed to dampen my spirits. I was on my way to a farm, and on that farm I was to learn homesteading skills worthy of Thoreau, worthy of the world as I knew it, which, according to the Mayans, was on its way out. But not even the imminent apocalypse—about which I'd been reading on the train—could demoralize me. In any case, the skills that I was on my way to learn would surely stand me in good stead after the cataclysm.

An hour or so into my hike, I spotted a woman weeding in her garden and stopped to ask for directions. When I told her where I was going and the name of the English woman with whom I would be staying, there was an almost indiscernible flicker in her face. She put down her tools, looked up and down the street as if making sure the coast was clear, and then half-invited, half-ushered me in for a *jus d'orange*.

For some reason, I often provoke tears of nostalgia in women of a certain age. And Madame Véry, as my new acquaintance was called, was no different. All I did was ask about her family who, it seemed, had all abandoned her. It was hard to tell whom she missed most: her dog and husband in the hereafter, or her son and daughter in Paris.

As moving as her tale was, it was not the information I'd been expecting to hear. It had seemed that she had wanted to tell me something, but no intelligence was forthcoming. Aware that the light was fading, and that I still had a few miles to walk, I made to leave. She reached for a pen, wrote down her number, and pressed it into my hand with an earnest "au cas où."

Just in case.

I pocketed the paper and went on my way, wondering if there was, indeed, something she had wanted to tell me. I was still wondering when I reached the hamlet, which was to be my new home. Of the dozen or so stone houses clustered on the side of the hill, no more than half looked habitable. Startled by the sound of a latch, I looked round to see a hunched figure emerging from a house several feet away. Either the stone-cobbled doorway was exceedingly small or else she was extremely large. As she regained her full height, I decided it was the latter. Large in a Matilda-facing-Trunchbull sort of way and with an uncertain smile to match. I imagine she supposed it to be welcoming, but I found it far from reassuring.

As I stepped into the warm house, all my concerns melted away. It was the fulfilment of all my rustic reveries: solid stone walls supported by rough-hewn beams, from which hung cast-iron pots in which we would make mouth-watering ragoûts, which we would eat at the solid wood table…My daydream was interrupted by an invitation to take a walk outside, to see where I would be spending most of my time. She told me that there was much to be done: beds to tend, compost to turn, animals to feed, milk, and finally slaughter.

We came back inside, and she brusquely closed and locked the door. Looking directly into my eyes, she asked me not to talk to the neighbors about the work I was doing.

Strange, I thought. *But maybe she just likes to keep herself to herself.*

"Actually, I don't want you to talk to them at all," she added, and reached for a chopping board and knife.

*

I slept fitfully that night, kept awake by the alarm bells in my head and the cowbells in the shed. The following morning, however, I was ready to get my hands dirty. I introduced myself to the animals, gathered walnuts from the meadow, and looked on as my hostess made goats' milk. This was exactly the post-apocalyptic preparation I'd been hoping for and, yet, I remained uneasy. Something wasn't right, but I still couldn't discern what it was.

My disquiet was only heightened by the non-appearance of the Belgians.

She had made mention of them on my first evening, a "lovely Belgian couple" who were due to arrive the following day to work through the winter. But they never showed up. When I asked about them, I was told in a *mind-your-own-business* tone:

"They'll be here tomorrow."

Tomorrow came and the compost was turned, the animals fed, the eggs collected—but no Belgians. Again, I asked and, again, the response was the same:

"Tomorrow…they should be here tomorrow."

*

The following afternoon, returning from the wood with baskets full of walnuts, I found myself alone. I set down my load and sat out front to enjoy the last of the day's sunshine. Within moments, a door opened across the street and out came a wrinkled, wispy-haired man.

"Bonjour," he offered.

"Bonjour, monsieur," I replied, standing to greet him.

We chatted for a moment, and he asked if I would like to come in. He told me he was watching the rugby and would be glad for the company. I wavered on my side of the street, hesitant to flout the rules of the house.

He threw me a questioning look. "Tu peux, tu sais."

You can.

That was the strange thing: I knew that I *could*—and yet I felt like I couldn't. It was as if there was some invisible force-field preventing me from leaving the front porch. Otherwise, why did crossing the road to talk to a frail old man suddenly seem like the most daring thing I had ever done?

It was then that I knew that something was definitely wrong. I glanced up and down the street and darted across the road.

Once safely inside, he poured me a strong drink, which I sipped gratefully. But as with Mme Véry, there seemed to be a reluctance to talk about what mattered. He talked instead about the Rugby World Cup, about his sister next door with whom he no longer spoke, and again about the Rugby World Cup. Mid-sentence, he paused, listening to something audible only to him.

"She's looking for you," he informed me.

I cocked my head, but still nothing. Then, without warning, an almighty pounding at the front door shook the entire house.

"Kevin!" she bellowed. "I know you're there; get back over here right now!"

My companion glanced at the silhouetted figure outside and then listlessly back at the TV. Something about his insouciance gave me confidence. I hollered back, as jauntily as possible:

"I'll be over shortly!"

One more drink and I made my way reluctantly across the street, wishing that my octogenarian friend were by my side.

I was greeted by a censorious tirade:

for working too slowly!
for stopping work when there was still more to be done!!
and, worst of all, for associating with the locals!!!

Before I had a chance to reply, she had stormed out of the house and down the road.

*

106

Now was my chance. I scrambled up the narrow wooden stairs to the sitting room and cautiously lifted the phone. Taking the now crumpled piece of paper from my pocket, I dialed the number.

Quivering with the fear of being found out, I whispered into the receiver.

"Allô, Mme Véry ? C'est Kevin, le…"

I was about to explain who Kevin was but there was no need. She told me she'd been expecting my call and that she would come first thing in the morning to take me to the station.

Relieved, I put down the phone, peered out through the dust-covered window to confirm that the street was still empty, and turned on the computer. I needed to make contact with some friends in Paris to see if I could stay the following night. I was just finishing up when I heard the familiar rattle from the front door echo through the old house.

I clicked *send* then *close* and then, to my horror, the computer froze.

"Please…please," I whispered, clicking frantically. I heard her mumbling to herself as she crossed the kitchen, filled the kettle, and mounted the stairs. By the time she reached the top, I was already on the sofa, leafing nonchalantly through a book.

I followed her back downstairs and we dined together in silence. I didn't bother asking about the Belgians because I knew that they weren't coming and probably never were. I though it better not to tell her of my intended departure, genuinely fearful of what might transpire during the night if I did.

*

When I awoke, she was already downstairs preparing breakfast. If she knew anything of my plans, she gave no indication and, instead, began talking about the day ahead. I heard a car approaching and, rising to my feet, informed her that I was leaving. I looked out the window and there she was, my *knightess* in her less than shining *Renault 5*.

With rescue imminent, I shook off the last of my timidity

and dashed upstairs to fetch my already-packed bag. I came back down to find the Trunchbull standing, hands on hips, by Mme Véry's car. The latter sat stiffly in her seat, hands clutching the wheel, staring straight ahead.

I went round and jumped in beside her. As we trundled off into the misty morning, I glanced back at the house opposite, where I thought I saw the slightest twitch of the curtain. I hadn't been able to say goodbye, but I knew that he was rejoicing with, and for, me.

*

Mme Véry and I had plenty of time before my train for a cup of tea and *pain au chocolat* at the local café. Intrigued by what she heard, the propriétaire came round from behind the counter to listen to my tale in full. And every new villager who arrived was beckoned over and I was requested to start again. Everyone had an opinion about *her*, but they were thirsty for *facts*. All of us agreed that something wasn't quite right, but none of us could quite put a finger on what, exactly, it was.

*

The mist was beginning to lift as my train pulled away from the station, Mme Véry waving all the while. I reached into my pocket and found the now crumpled piece of paper inscribed with her number. I pressed it flat, folded it, and tucked it into my wallet.

Au cas où. Just in case.

CATHY HAS VISITORS

William Quincy Belle

Cathy pulled her wheeled shopping basket down the street from the bus stop. It had been three years since she and Tom had given up their car, but so far they had managed to live without it. There were a few inconveniences from having to rely on public transit, but generally people had been helpful. That bus driver had been very nice when he offered to carry her basket off the bus. Yes, Cathy and Tom had given up a bit of their freedom, but they were getting up in years and, with things being tight with their pensions, it was good to not be spending money on a car for gas, maintenance, and insurance. Every dollar counted.

Speaking of every dollar, the grocery store had their steaks on sale so Cathy decided to splurge. Tom was going to be tickled pink when he got a look at tonight's dinner. Add in some fried mushrooms and a baked potato and the two of them were going to have a meal fit for a king. Oh, and a queen. Cathy smiled to herself at her little joke. It was fun making themselves out to be a royal couple. Ha, ha.

Cathy unlatched the metal mesh gate and pulled her basket onto the walkway. She turned around to shut the gate and make sure that it was securely in place. Last week, she had looked out the window to discover the gate wide open and two dogs running around their yard. Maybe Tom had not closed it properly. Then again, it could have been her. She'd be more careful.

Stepping around the basket, Cathy took the handle and started pulling it up the walk. When she got to the steps leading to the front porch, she stepped ahead of the basket and carefully pulled it up and over each step. She might not be able to lift the loaded basket, but with a little finesse she could wheel it up and down stairs. Once the basket was over the last step and on the porch itself, Cathy stopped for a moment to catch her breath. She looked up and down the street. A few children were visible in a yard a few doors down, but it was relatively quiet. They were the oldest couple on the street, Cathy and Tom, Grandma and Grandpa. Well, they were grandparents to their own grandkids, but being the last of the previous generation in the neighborhood made Cathy realize just how long they had lived in their house.

Cathy sighed. She then turned to the front door and pulled open the screen door. She opened the heavy wooden front door and, holding the screen door with one hand, pulled the basket around her into the house. Cathy let the screen door shut on its automatic closer. She pulled the basket out of the way and shut the front door.

Cathy spoke up, "Tom?" Cathy took off her coat and hung it up. She wondered where her husband had gotten off to. "Tom?" Cathy listened. It was quiet. She picked up her purse and took two steps in the hall to the double doors that led into the living room. The doors were always open and Cathy thought the last time they had ever closed the doors was when all the kids came to visit with their families two years ago. They didn't have enough beds for everybody, so the living room had turned into a makeshift bedroom.

She stood looking into the living room, not believing her eyes. Tom was sitting in a wooden straight-back chair in the middle of the room with a pillowcase over his head. His hands had been taped to the arms of the chair and his legs were taped to the front legs. "Tom?" Cathy stepped towards her husband. She held her purse up and grasped the handle with both hands, a look of complete bewilderment on her face.

The next thing Cathy remembered was being face down on the floor. She had no idea how she got there. She had no idea what happened. Did she faint? She heard unfamiliar voices.

"What the hell did you do that for?"

Cathy didn't recognize the voice.

"I thought she was going for her purse." This voice was a little deeper than the first voice.

"So?" The voice sounded angry.

"I thought she might have been going for her cell phone. Maybe to phone the police?" The last sentence took the form of a question as the voice seemed to asking forgiveness from the first person.

"What?" There was a twinge of exasperation in the voice. After a pause, the voice resumed with a calmer tone. "Lennie, how much do you weigh?"

There was a moment of silence as the person seemingly tried to understand how this new topic of conversation was pertinent to the discussion. "Ah, two hundred and forty?" Once again the deeper voice sounded unsure. Where was this going?

"And how much do you think the old woman weighs?"

There was some movement of feet on the floor. The deeper voice was fidgeting a bit. "I dunno. A hundred?"

"So, that means you outweigh her by one hundred and forty pounds." The higher voice coughed. "You are nearly a foot taller than her. You are stronger than her. If you thought she was going to go for her cellphone, why didn't you just take the purse from her?"

There was a moment of silence. "You said they shouldn't see our faces, George."

"I ...." The higher voice trailed off. It would seem that Lennie had made a point that George couldn't refute. "Get the other pillowcase!" commanded George.

Cathy felt the cloth being pulled over her head. She was still dazed from the open-handed slap which had knocked her to the ground. Hands grabbed her arms and lifted her off the floor. She was forced into a chair, and she heard tape being pulled off a roll. Cathy clenched her fists as somebody wrapped tape around her forearms and her ankles. She was securely fixed to the chair.

"That's enough. Now let's go see if we can find their stash." Cathy heard the steps creak as the men went upstairs. It was quiet for a moment, then some muffled noises came from somewhere overhead.

Cathy turned to her right and whispered, "Tom! Tom! Are you all right?"

"I'm here, Cathy," said her husband.

Cathy turned and continued whispering. "What the heck is going on? Who are these men?"

"I have no idea. I never saw them. One minute I was walking into the living room, the next minute I was being grabbed from behind and having a hood put over my head. I'm guessing I'm taped to a dining room chair."

"That's what it looked like before ... before ...."

"Before what? I heard something like a slap. Did they hit you? You fell on the floor?"

"I guess ... yes. My right cheek is pretty sore right now. But what do they want?"

Cathy could see some light and dark through the material of the pillowcase. She thought she could see the outline of her husband next to her.

"They haven't talked too much in front of me, but from what little I've heard, and from what they just said, they seem to think we have something valuable here in the house."

"Like what?"

"I have no idea. Either they have gotten faulty information from somewhere or they have come to the wrong house. Whatever the case, they are determined to search the premises."

"But what are they going to do when they find out we don't have anything of value? Are they going to kill us?"

"I'd like to say no, but I'm not sure at this point. Although I haven't heard any mention of guns."

"They don't necessarily need a gun to kill us."

"They've put pillowcases over our heads so we can't see them. Somehow, that makes me think they don't want murder on their hands. Up to now, this has just been a robbery. Maybe they are not prepared to go to the next level."

"The big one hit me, well, slapped me. If they don't find what they're after, they may get angry with us." Cathy leaned closer. "Tom, I'm scared."

Tom leaned closer, too. "We're going to make it, Cathy."

Cathy strained to touch Tom. She pulled on the tape around her right hand. It yielded slightly. Cathy sat back up. She twisted her right arm. The sticky part of the tape pulled at her skin, but she managed to turn her arm slightly. There was a certain looseness to the tape. It seemed as if her clenching her fists had kept her arm up a bit off the arm of the chair so the man didn't tape her tightly to the chair. She had a little room to move.

"Tom, my arm is a bit loose." Cathy twisted her arm back and forth, trying to rotate it under the tape.

"Can you get out? I've tried several times, but they did a good job taping me."

"Maybe." Cathy's twisting had freed her arm from the stickiness of the tape, and now she was trying to pull it back under the tape. She twisted her arm some more and tried pulling again. The tape was tight around her hand, but she kept pulling, hoping the tape would stretch. "I might be able to get it." Cathy twisted, then pulled again. She grunted with the effort, but she could feel her hand slipping slowly through the tape.

All of a sudden, her hand popped out. "I got my right hand out." Cathy immediately reached up and yanked the pillowcase off of her head. She blinked for a moment and looked at her husband. "Give me a second to get free." She set to work trying to free her left hand. It took a moment to locate the end of the tape, then she began to unwind it from the arm of the chair.

Cathy could hear the men searching the rooms upstairs. Drawers were being opened and there was occasionally movement between the rooms. How much time did she have?

Cathy leaned over and started unraveling the tape around her legs. This part was much easier.

A voice from upstairs yelled, "Lennie?"

"Yeah."

"Did you hear something?"

"Hear what?"

"Go downstairs and check on those people." Distinct steps could be heard coming down the hall to the stairs.

Cathy panicked. She took off the last bit of tape and hurried out of the chair and across the room. She looked around madly and spied a large cut glass vase on the dining room table. It was substantial and heavy. She picked it up, then stepped behind one of the living room doors. Steps were coming down the stairs.

They stopped just outside in the hall. "What?" The voice sounded surprised. The larger man with the deep voice walked into the living room towards Tom. "Hey, mister, where did that woman go?"

Cathy walked up behind the man and swung the vase. It hit the back of the man's head with a resounding thunk and sort of bounced off the skull. For a moment, the man didn't move. Had Cathy knocked him out? The man slowly turned towards Cathy. He seemed to be unaffected by the blow. Or was he dazed?

Cathy wound up and swung the vase up and around and brought it crashing down on the man's forehead with all the force she could muster. This time, though, the vase slammed into the skull and broke into several pieces. The man's eyes rolled back in his head and he fell. He didn't move. Was he dead?

A voice from upstairs screamed, "Lennie? Lennie?" Mad footsteps came running down the hall and started trampling down the stairs. "Lennie? Lennie?"

The man arrived at the foot of the stairs and could see into the living room. "Lennie!" He ran forward and saw his large friend lying on the floor with broken glass around him. "You bitch!" He angrily let out a backhand and caught Cathy on her right cheek, the same cheek Lennie had hit earlier. Cathy fell backwards from the force of the blow and hit the floor.

George looked at Lennie. "Lennie?" George leaned over. "Lennie?" There was no response. George turned to Cathy and hissed, "You better not have killed him." However, Cathy had already gotten up and was starting towards the living room doors. George madly reached out to grab her, but only managed to partially get a hold of some clothing. There was a ripping sound, then Cathy lost her balance and fell forward onto the floor in the hall. George stomped forward. "You bitch. You're going to pay for that."

Cathy was panicking. She crawled a few steps, then turned back to face George, frightened about what he might do. She crawled backward into a stand of umbrellas and boots and everything came crashing onto the floor in a clatter. George stepped forward, his face red with anger. He pointed at Cathy and yelled, "Damn you!"

George went to leap onto Cathy. Cathy reached to one side and picked up an umbrella as a weapon. She held it with the point out towards George. George jumped, and the point hit the middle of his chest just to the right of the breast bone. The weight of George's body drove all four inches of the umbrella point into his chest. The look of anger on George's face turned into utter surprise. There was a moment when George was suspended over Cathy on the shaft of the umbrella. Then, the balance changed and George fell to the floor on his side, the umbrella still embedded in his chest. Cathy stared at him, shaking with fright. George's eyes were wide, saucer shaped, glazed over in surprise or pain. He was looking right at Cathy, but it was like he wasn't looking at her at all.

Cathy pulled away and jumped up. She slowly backed away, staring in shock at the man and the umbrella sticking through his shirt into his chest. George was shaking and making gurgling sounds. Was he dying?

Cathy ran back into the living room. She pulled the pillowcase off of her husband's head. "Oh, Tom." She threw her arms around her husband.

"The police, Cathy, the police!" he whispered. Cathy yanked at the tape around Tom's left arm. "That's enough! That's enough! Phone the police immediately!"

Cathy saw that Tom could continue on his own, so she ran to the kitchen phone and dialed 9-1-1. As soon as somebody answered, she excitedly said in a low voice, "We're being robbed! 285 Greendale Avenue. The men are still in the house. Send the police!"

When Tom finally released himself, he and Cathy ran down the front steps of their house, down the length of the walk, out of the gate, and down the street, trying to put as much distance as possible between them and the house. They both saw a police cruiser turn onto their street and started waving their arms and yelling.

The next day, the newspaper ran a front-page story about the two robbers who were subdued by a seventy-eight-year-old lady. A photo showed the two bad guys being wheeled out of the house on stretchers, the bigger man having suffered a concussion and the smaller one sustaining a stab wound. The article concluded with a report from the police that the men had confessed to trying to steal what they'd been told was a stash of gold in an upstairs room.

"Gold?" Cathy said to Tom as they read the article at their kitchen table. "The only people we know who keep gold in their home are the Hendersons next door... Oh...!"

UPRISINGS AT CAP D'ANTIBES

Robert Mangeot

The white blur came out of the French sunlight, rebounded off the clay, and rocketed straight for me. The vague impression of a tennis ball whizzed past my ear. Behind me, the chain link fence shivered from high-velocity impact.

Off the court, in Hailey's neon outfits and sudden grins, I still glimpsed the girl who'd never brush her mother back with a forehand smash. On the court, she turned into a predator, twelve going on twenty-five.

I rediscovered breathing and said, "Your dad wants us working on your backhand."

Hailey bounced on her toes. "So make me hit one."

"I'm trying," I whispered, but my next try caught the racket frame, arced over the fence, and rolled twenty meters of Côte d'Azur lawn away.

Hailey moved on to serves, and I wandered out after my miscue. Feliks Karperov Academy was as posh as advertised: tournament stadium, seaside dorms, state-of-the-art workout room, citrus trees and royal palms. "Molding talent into elite since 1992," his website boasted. "Where French glitz meets Grand Slams," *Topspin Magazine* proclaimed. "The Karperovs choose their students," my husband Tom swore. "Feliks has a shoe deal," Hailey added.

Bonding time, I had thought. Tom, the ex-jock, covered Hailey's practices and conditioning, but closing a development loan for lakefront housing would keep him in Louisville all spring. I jumped at the chance for a serious mother-daughter adventure of glam beaches and harbor villages.

A buff-white Pomeranian shot around me and snatched up

the tennis ball. The dog squared its body my way, as if daring me to do something about it.

"Keep it," I said.

The dog, top-heavy with its prize, trotted a half-circle over to Feliks Karperov, now courtside and watching Hailey rip serves. The old champ had been unavailable when we checked in the day before—"much of the illnesses," his son Sergei had said—and, when I asked again that morning, Sergei warned me not to instigate. That sent me slinking out of the clubhouse. My closest to instigator was my fame among the junior competition parents for mixing the best cocktails.

I moved in breezing Feliks my tennis circuit smile, friendly but not overdone. "Dasha Meacham, Hailey's mom."

He pressed my hand into a kiss. Age had worn on the man I'd seen in his sailboat racing photos, but if vigor and eyebrow heft were any gauge, the champ had plenty of sets left in him.

"Hailey's got a cannonball, huh?" I said. "She keeps us shopping for trophy shelves."

Feliks nodded to his dog sniffing along the fence. "Is Gorbachev. Like Soviet premier."

I'd take his word for it. Despite my family tree, I was as Russian as my Tanqueray gimlets.

"The Pomeranian," Feliks said. "Noble animal. Once as large as the wolf. Did you know this?"

"Is that right?"

"Bred down. They take out the wolf, make it toy. Something for handbags."

"He's a cutie."

Feliks knitted his brow, or he might have under all that brow hair. "We speak of dogs, but this is metaphor, yes?"

"For tennis?"

Hailey smacked a ball into the net and let loose a word Tom must have taught her.

"For revolution," Feliks said.

Revolution topped my max for creepy metaphors. I seized on the first conversational out available, Sergei and two security guys hurrying up to the fence.

"You are a pig," Sergei hissed at his father. "A bloated, capitalist swine ordered to remain in his pen."

I asked if everything was okay, and Sergei wheeled around to me, all hawk's nose and glower. His eyes crackled with menace. "Your Academy pass."

"But we just spoke—"

"Academy pass."

I tucked down my hair. "It's in my gym bag."

Sergei made a note of that, nothing good either based on the piercing look he aimed over his clipboard. One security guy latched onto me, the other onto Feliks.

"See?" Feliks said. "Now Dasha must be wolf."

*

Sergei had me escorted off Academy grounds, citing a rule about no parents or media during instruction time. Really, his beady eyes declared, he meant no instigators.

The whole episode sucked any joy out of an afternoon at the hotel pool. Instead, I donned a sun hat and went Côte d'Azur native. Roaming through old Antibes and sniffing hyacinths at the flower market cleared my head, but less and less in a pleasant way. Hailey's workshop that night, reprogramming the mind for victory, took on darker possibilities.

I stopped at a promenade café with a quiet corner to phone Tom. His admin picked up and promised she'd find him for me.

Across the harbor, the cliffs of Cap d'Antibes bulged out into the aquamarine sea. Hailey and I were supposed to be up there, enjoying a tour of the Karperov villa, goggling at movie stars, and generally connecting through extreme *savoir vivre*. Instead, she might undergo a leftist brainwashing.

Tom called back during my second glass of Vin de Pays. I recounted the afternoon, to which he said: "Das, breathe. It's just an old guy off his meds. And Sergei, he's European. Radical there is like our hipsters. Anyway, you're talking about a tennis camp."

"Sergei's a total communist."

"Used to be, big time. Last of the Soviet tennis poster boys. Feliks was a Russian idol in his day. Just tell me those damn commies like Hailey's game."

"You weren't there," I said. "It's like a coup. That Sergei has the eeriest stare since Rasputin."

"The bearded guy? Was he even communist?"

"I don't know!"

"Look, I'll talk to Sergei. In the meantime, just don't freak out Hailey. I want her hyper-focused."

I'd have thought a banking exec would take revolution more seriously, bankers supposedly first up against the wall, but Tom said goodbye and went back to funding lakefront McMansions.

*

That night, the guard at the Academy gatehouse asked for my passport and club card. He checked his list and, what I had assumed was his permanent frown, deepened into a scowl.

"Visit tomorrow," he said. "After the lunchtime."

"I have a right to see my daughter."

The guard waved me off. "Parents tomorrow. CENTACAD orders."

I stayed put, hands locked on the wheel. Stalemated, the guy made a show of dialing CENTACAD or whoever on his phone. A clipped exchange later, he opened the gate.

Any trace of Feliks had been purged from the Academy grounds. Placards lauded impossibly robust tennis players in dramatic poses, including Sergei in his Olympic glory.

Hailey waited for me on the clubhouse steps, looking tan and capitalist girl chic in a tank top and Capri pants. She wriggled out of my hug. "God, Mom. What's wrong?"

"I didn't get a chance to say goodbye earlier—"

"You so got busted."

"—and I'm dying to hear how your day went."

"Control drills and then volleys and footwork. Sergei is this amazing coach."

"What about tonight? The mental part?"

Hailey shrugged. "I don't know. Kind of weird. It started out all the usual no fear and performance state stuff. Then Sergei got all 'Western kids are fat and weak' and broke us into groups. Me and some others, he wants in this inner circle. For top players, so that's cool."

"No, honey. I'm pretty sure it's a communist thing."

"I guess. This Dutch kid asked about the shoe deal and where's Feliks, and Sergei just went off about oppressor cabals exploiting everybody."

"This place isn't right for you, honey. We'll call your father from the hotel."

"I already talked to Dad. Hey, bring cash tomorrow. He says its suicides every serve I don't break and, if you pay the security guys, you get extra Powerade."

*

Back in my room, I managed not to cry through another pointless call with Tom, who had convinced himself communist connections might improve Hailey's odds at an Ivy League scholarship. I took matters into my own hands, researching communist theory over the hotel's pay-by-the-minute Internet. The bill might get Tom's attention if revolution didn't, and, like Hailey studied her opponents, so would I.

The proletariat, Lenin wrote, must throw off its shackles and form its own dictatorship to prevent capitalists from regaining power. Replacing the old elite, he posited a new one, a Party vanguard that chopped off any toe not in collective line.

From my laptop, Lenin's arched face glowered out at posterity. I said, "Good thing you were in the vanguard, huh?"

Later, my phone rang as I moped in front of the computer. I took out some frustration punching the receive button. "Hello?"

A click, then white noise.

"Hello?"

"Darya Eduardovna Meacham." A man. A statement, not a greeting. "You were warned agitating is unwise. Poisoning family against the cause is unwise. Do not attempt this again."

"Being a mother is not agitating."

A tiger's smile crept into his monotone. "Ah, but mothers seek what is best for child. Puberty, it changes everything in the tennis player. The girl must have firm instruction or performance window is lost. Pity the mother who obstructs this. Consider these lessons carefully, Darya Eduardovna."

*

The sun had worked up to a mid-morning bake when I arrived at Karperov Academy. The club pass I showed the gatehouse guy came wrapped in a hundred euro note. I came wrapped in a stretchy black turtleneck that hopefully screamed leftist. The guard let me through, no production made of dialing the clubhouse.

Overnight, the placards had spread like cartoonish mold over the stucco walls. The new star amid Sergei's idealized youth was my daughter: Hailey brandishing her racket, Hailey coiled in a serve toss, Hailey in mid-backhand and owning the baseline.

Most courts sat open. Party members only, a sign said. Trainers had the kids jogging or practicing on the lawn. I didn't see Hailey, but there was no Sergei either, and that told me where to start looking.

At center court, another fifty euro put Hailey in unlimited Powerade, and twenty more bought a shady seat in my usual domain, the bleachers. Down on the court, Sergei crouched hands on knees, barking at Hailey while she blasted unreturnable serves. Hailey spotted me and, on her next serve, bellowed out a grunt that rang through the stadium. The ball clipped the net and spun long.

Sergei drew up, as if about to unleash an epic reprimand. Our eyes met, which made my skin ready to crawl off to a safe house and made him signal an assistant coach. He switched Hailey to light hitting, volleying her sideline to sideline. Her stroke fizzed with new power, an assassin's fizz.

Soon, intellectual types began to fill the courtside boxes. The vanguard, I wondered, or a chess club. I was picturing them in old-time tennis wear when my phone vibrated. A serious tennis mom faux pas, but Sergei kept his clipboard holstered. I checked the number—Tom, no surprise—and turned the phone off. Only then did Sergei seem irritated.

Hailey grabbed a towel and climbed the bleachers up to me. "You look like a slutty English teacher."

I showed off my beatnik sweater. "Just trying to blend."

"Mom, stop," Hailey said, stifling a grin. She knocked back some bootleg Powerade. "I'm playing this girl Erika next. The winner gets invited to a thing at Sergei's villa tonight."

Not that I enjoyed rooting against my daughter, but the idea flared up anyway. "Yeah? Is she any good?"

"Chicken at the net. I will destroy her. Come watch from Sergei's box. The thing I like about communism is you get privileges."

*

Courtside, the privileges abounded: champagne, finger foods, socca bread fresh off the coals. The luxury set-up reminded me of nights helping Tom entertain clients at the bank's arena suite, but instead of his chamber of commerce buddies, I had wild-haired intellectuals getting socca crumbs in their beards.

Sergei found the seat beside mine. He eyed me ice picks and said, "Sweater does not make a radical."

"Peace, okay?" Peace until I hog-tied and dragged Hailey to the airport. Until then, it was sip and schmooze. "I admit you all have style. I mean, you couldn't have picked a nicer spot to start a revolution."

Sergei munched hard on a stuffed mushroom and gestured for the umpire to start the match.

Poor undersized Erika fired off the opening serve. Hailey volleyed back a winner loaded with killer intent, her war grunt igniting a charge of excitement around the stadium. So went the entire match. Hailey dominated the net and peppered ace after ace, Erika flailed against the barrage, and the vanguard thrilled at the display.

"Yes," the intellectual behind me said. "She is the spearhead."

Hailey capped the two-set, double bagel demolition with a teasing drop shot that left Erika gawking on the baseline.

The intellectual leaned in with a conspiratorial whisper. "First, Hailey Fominincha. Then those who want to be her. Then more camps, more sports, the Olympics, adoring masses. Your daughter makes a most excellent icon."

No, I thought, Hailey of the shoe-deal fetish made them a horrible icon, a spectacular crash and burn no matter how their revolution ended.

*

At dusk, Sergei escorted Hailey and me into his Mercedes. We pulled out past Erika, now among the kids practicing on the lawn. They had assigned her a wooden racket.

The car climbed up narrow lanes into Cap d'Antibes. Near the swank Eden Roc hotel, we entered Sergei's compound overlooking the harbor and rugged Mediterranean coast. In the marinas below, sailboat lights bobbed with the tide.

Once inside the villa, Sergei whisked Hailey into his film room, leaving me in a salon full of trophies and Soviet memorabilia. Strains of folk guitar and accordion filtered in from the terrace pool. I stepped outside and stood there observing the aging militants who had staked a claim on my daughter.

Then I thought, if everyone shaved and the ratty sport coats were blazers instead, I had attended dozens of events like this, tennis people gathered around a torch-lit pool and chatting over drinks. Tonight was one more party where nobody cared about Hailey beyond the prodigy slice of her. I had launched Hailey's rocket ride, and I owed joining in on her crash.

If she wanted to be a Party icon, so be it. No one in youth tennis worked a party like Darya Eduardovna.

For a half-hour, I mingled, giving Sergei's crew the tennis mom smile, complimenting ideas, squeezing arms, nodding along. First impression made, I sent the bartender for limes and grabbed the cranberry juice and vodka. By the time Sergei and Hailey arrived to great applause, everyone on the terrace sipped my Cape Cods, tonight repackaged as Red Menaces.

Hailey waved to me and wormed over through her fan club. Sergei had her decked out in an Academy tracksuit, as if anyone could miss the Amazonian tween among musty radicals.

"It's official," I said, sliding her a cranberry and lime. "We're going revolutionary together. I'll be good at it, too. You know I will."

Hailey's eyes popped wide. "Dad would kill you."

"Honey, that's going to work the other way around."

"Whatever. Everybody here is old. Oh, and Sergei is cancelling Feliks' shoe deal. Symbols of the oppressor. He's got this new South American company. Their shoes are hideous." She fingered her jacket sleeve. "He says I have to wear this. Do I have to wear this?"

A flash of white fur caught my eye. Across the terrace, the Pomeranian ran past the cabana and into a formal garden.

"Take Sergei his drink," I said. "And really push him on the shoe deal, okay?"

It took a minute to break away unnoticed, but I slipped down the footpath where Gorbachev had vanished.

"*Dobryj vyechyer*," said someone in the gloom between cypresses, Feliks based on the bushy eyebrows discernable anywhere. He leaned out and clapped his approval. "Way to step it up. Not she-wolf, but better."

"How are you?"

"Ha! Fit as team of horses. I have boat in harbor. You get girl, boom boom boom, Majorca."

"You are so hired."

I bided my time broaching the getaway with Hailey, content to let Sergei rant at her about class friction reaching critical mass. When he paused for breath, I swooped in with a fresh round of drinks.

"Your Red Menace could use a comrade," I said.

Sergei took a pull and said, "Cocktail does not make radical."

"Well, I have to start somewhere."

I made a vague excuse about female issues and led Hailey off to the powder room. "Sweetie," I said when locked inside, "would you like to get out of here?"

"Can we? Everyone is kind of pervy and has cigarette breath."

Fifteen minutes later, I eased Hailey down from the bathroom window. A loyalist stashed us in the trunk of his car, and we rode in darkness to the marina. In short order, Feliks had us aboard his Twister yacht and cruising out of Antibes harbor. I stayed at the bow, dog sitting. Gorbachev quivered with excitement, his nose windward and testing the salt air.

Hailey proved a quick study as first mate. I waited until

she had secured the lines and riggings to call out an overdue question. "Do you even like tennis anymore?"

"Most days. But some girls at camp were taking dance lessons, like for ballrooms. I want to start, too."

"You like dancing? Since when?"

"Since always," she said. "Were you going to go commie?"

"*Da*, kiddo. You're stuck with me."

There we were, Hailey and I fleeing across the Mediterranean with a deposed tennis champ and his pocket wolf. Maybe we would fly home. Maybe not. Hell, I was instigating now, so maybe we'd help start the counterrevolution. Tonight, with the moon reflected gold on the glassy water, it was enough that we kept on sailing

RESCUE IN THE MYSTICAL MOUNTAINS

C.B. Heinemann

As soon as I saw them I felt in my gut that going up into them would somehow alter my life. Rising abruptly from the Rio Lebregat valley northwest of Barcelona, the gnarled teeth of the Montserrat mountain range seemed to hang from the clouds rather than spring from the earth. Monks and mystics once withdrew from the world to meditate and pray among those peaks. Today, more tourists than mystics visit the weirdly magnificent mountains that look like geological anomalies from another planet.

"I've never felt such an odd sensation about visiting a place," said my wife, Annette. "According to legend, Parsifal found the Holy Grail up there somewhere, and Saint Peter hid a carving of the Black Madonna in a cave—the same Black Madonna they have in the monastery's basilica."

"I know, that's one reason I want to go there—I've never seen one of those Black Madonnas. Nobody knows who made any of them, or even when."

"You were certainly insistent about coming. Maybe the Black Madonna was calling to you."

I laughed. "Maybe. Aren't you glad now that we came?"

We corkscrewed up a vertical road and entered the village of Montserrat where it clings to the side of the mountains. We then parked and walked past the sprawling monastery to Plaza Santa Noria, where the basilica and one of Spain's finest art museums, Museu de Montserrat, sit on the edge of the square. Following a string of pilgrims, we entered the vast basilica and approached the altar from a side aisle. From there we entered a dark viewing room to have a close look at the famous Madonna. With her solemn expression and dazzling gold dress, she gazed serenely across the centuries into my eyes. I experienced a subtle but distinctly odd sensation. "These Catholics love their dolls," I said, trying to make light of it. "I guess all the wealth of Spain went into dressing them up while poor people went hungry."

The Museu was a delight, featuring works by El Greco, Picasso, and other artists. But already I was beginning to feel the gravitational pull of the high mountains just on the edge of town. I always had problems with heights, but an inexplicable urgency prodded me to run over and buy tickets for the funicular that would take us high into the mountains. I ran back to the car to bring a couple of tins of lamb stew even though we already had sandwiches in my daypack. I had no inkling that we were about to embark on our own mystical adventure.

After drinking in the dizzying view from the upper funicular station, we followed a path past massive rock formations, through wooded areas, and along steep ridges with incredible views. After a look at the derelict Monastery of Sant Joan, we trudged uphill to the remote hermitage of Sant Jeronino, one of many scattered through the mountains. The lonely peaks around us had been sculpted into eerie shapes by centuries of wind and rain.

I decided to follow a narrow path that led us above the trees to the highest point in the Montserrat range. The fierce winds pounded us and an attack of vertigo forced me to sit down for a few minutes. "We can go back if you need to," Annette said. "But I think you'll regret it. These views are amazing!"

That internal sense of urgency compelled me to get up and keep going, ignoring my fear. We ascended a stairway cut into the stone, clinging to an ancient iron handrail to keep from being blown off the mountain. By the time we reached the tiny platform at the very top, I felt like I'd climbed a tower to the clouds, and couldn't force myself to look down. I had to sit down again and stare at the ground to regain my composure.

A man sat reading on a nearby rock, and he greeted us in English. I glanced up and noticed that we shared the platform with two small beagles, a mother and her pup, who sat tied to the railing and huddled together against the wind.

"Are those your dogs?" I asked.

The man looked up from his book. "I don't know who they belong to. I've come up here to read the past couple of days, and they've been here both times."

"You mean somebody just left them up here?"

"It looks that way. I've brought them food and water, but I can't get them to come down with me."

Two little dogs, deserted on a windblown mountaintop! How could anybody leave their pets to starve there alone, especially in an area so steeped in spirituality? Annette and I petted them while they moved closer to get warm. We knew immediately what we had to do.

Annette turned to the man. "We've got to get them down. Otherwise they'll just die up here."

"But how will you get them down? They're too weak to walk."

My vertigo was forgotten and I stood up. "I'll carry them if I have to. We can't just leave them here."

I took a tin of stew from my daypack, opened it up, and placed it on the ground. The dogs gobbled it up in a moment. We then untied the dogs and held out some more pieces of meat from the other tin. After some coaxing, they began to follow us.

Our hike back became a more arduous trek than I anticipated. The mother dog was too weak to walk, so I had to carry her in my arms. The pup was more energetic, and frisked around our legs. The only other hiker we encountered was an American who donated his bottle of water to the two dehydrated dogs after hearing of their plight.

By the time we reached the funicular station later that afternoon, the mother dog was completely exhausted and her eyes were lifeless. The driver told us that after he dropped the last passengers at the bottom, he would return and take us and the dogs down into town. He left a plate of leftover pasta for the dogs before he left. We waited for more than an hour, but he never returned. As darkness surrounded us, we realized that we would have to walk back. I didn't know if I could carry the mother much longer, but I had to try.

Down and down we hiked as the sky became streaked with orange and purple. After some more food, water, and a rest, the mother was finally able walk on her own. We walked quickly to avoid becoming lost in the darkness. When we finally neared the town, the pup galloped ahead of us to stop and look at something. When we caught up with him, we saw that he was staring at a statue that had been built into a small grotto. A closer look revealed that he had been transfixed by a statute of St. Francis. The mother dog walked over to join her pup, and the two walked slowly and deliberately to the foot of the statue, their eyes on the face of St. Francis.

"Those two little dogs look like they're praying to Saint Francis," Annette whispered. "What do you think of the 'dolls' now?"

We all stood for several minutes while the dogs gazed into the face of the saint. It had to be more than mere coincidence—we had traveled a long way with those two, but that was the first time they did anything like that. The hairs on the back of my neck rose, and a chill squirmed through me.

As darkness completed its descent over the mountains, the dogs were ready to move on. We found the local police station and brought the dogs inside. An officer who spoke English took them, assuring us that the monks would adopt the two and take good care of them. He let us come with him to the monastery, where he put them into a large cage. Tears poured down Annette's face, and my own eyes began to fill with liquid.

"Don't worry, don't worry," the officer repeated. "They will be well cared for. My cousin runs a restaurant just around the corner. I'll bring them food right away. They'll only be in the cage for tonight."

With heavy hearts we left our two new friends behind. We had to wonder if we had somehow been led there that day to rescue the dogs. Why did I feel such a compulsion to go up to the top of Montserrat that day in spite of my fear of heights? Why bring tins of stew along though we didn't need them ourselves? Why did we climb to that part of the mountain and force ourselves to go on in spite of vertigo and strong winds? And why did the dogs stop to stand at the feet of the statue of St. Francis?

The mountains of Montserrat have long been home to mysteries, miracles, and legend, and after that day, they gave us something of a mystery of our own.

A CONVERSATION WITH JAY PARINI

Lowestoft Chronicle, March 2014

Jay Parini (Photography: Oliver Parini)

An avid writer for more than forty years—his first book, a volume of poetry, was published while he was still an undergraduate student—Jay Parini has authored dozens of books, from bestselling novels like *The Last Station*, which was turned into an Academy Award-nominated film, to widely praised poetry collections like *Anthracite Country*, described as "superb" in *The Sunday Times* and "a remarkable book" in the *Library Journal*. He has also written critically-acclaimed biographies of John Steinbeck, Robert Frost, William Faulkner, and Jesus, and edited many volumes of anthologies and literary criticism. His biography, *Robert Frost: A Life*, won the Chicago Tribune Heartland Prize for best non-fiction book of the year.

In a recent interview with *Lowestoft Chronicle*, Jay Parini discussed his poetry, his latest biography, and those early days of his writing career studying overseas in Scotland.

Lowestoft Chronicle [LC]: I remember you saying that you started off as a poet, your first love was poetry, and you consider yourself primarily a poet. You published your first book, *Singing in Time*, in 1972, while you were an undergraduate student at the University of St. Andrews. What made you decide to study in Scotland in the first place, and what made you want to remain there? Was Starglow Press (the publisher of that first book of poetry) a small independent press or was it university run?

Jay Parini [JP]: I went to Scotland for various reasons. Mainly, it was to get away from the US during the Vietnam War era. I felt threatened by my draft board, and I felt disenchanted with this country. I also had a kind of fantasy about Britain— had read so much literature set there, that I wanted to see for myself. I needed to get away is the short summary. And I did. Seven years there. I loved it, mostly. Nobody loves everything all the time, but Scotland was pretty much a good experience and often a great one. Met such interesting people, and learned so much. The little press that published my first poems was an independent and short-lived press in Fife. I knew the guy who ran it, a local bookseller. He did a few books then folded. But I very much thought of myself as ONLY a poet.

LC: You always begin each morning by writing poetry. You turn to fiction and criticism only after you've finished with your poetry for the day. *Anthracite Country*, your next book of poetry, wasn't published until 1982. Was the reason for this because you wanted to focus on other forms of literature or because of publishing commitments with Little, Brown & Company and Scribner, etc.?

JP: Poems take a long time for me. Unlike prose, which I write easily and swiftly. I don't like to rush a poem. I like them to

ANTHRACITE
COUNTRY
POEMS

JAY PARINI

Anthracite Country
Random House, 1982

sit for a long time. I figure that if, in a lifetime, I write a dozen good poems, that is enough. So that's my goal. I really only bring out a volume once every decade or so. More or less. Of course, the prose projects get in the way; all of the criticism, novels, biography, and other things take up writing time. I don't think I could, in fact, just focus on poems. I need the room in my head for lots of projects. I like that feeling of abundance.

LC: While teaching at Dartmouth College, you started getting poems published in *The New Yorker* and *The Atlantic*. You also co-founded the quarterly literary magazine, *New England Review*. When did you start sending out your work, Jay? What was the first piece you had published? And what made you decide to start a literary journal? Do you have much interaction with the magazine anymore?

JP: My first poem appeared in *Scottish International*, no longer in existence. I remember that day with great joy. I don't even remember what poem they published, however. Probably one I no longer even own. I had poems in *The New Yorker*, *The Atlantic*, and *Poetry* in the same year. Maybe 1978. Something like that. I sent poems to all the quarterlies, etc., and published in most of them: *Hudson*, *Sewanee*, *VQR*, *Paris Review*, and *Yale Review*. I don't pursue publication anymore; not in that way. Once in a while, I feel moved to send a poem somewhere, but usually not. I have only a very peripheral involvement with *New England Review*, which, of course, I co-founded. The editors are good friends now.

LC: I've heard you tell a great story about James Atlas approaching you to contribute to the ICONS biography series and, when you proposed to write one about Jesus, he almost fell off his seat. Prior to writing the biography, I know you originally intended to write a novel about Christ. Having done so much research into his life, will you be putting your notes toward a novel at a later date?

JP: That's a true story. Jim Atlas almost fainted when I suggested Jesus as a topic. He had suggested Sofya Tolstoy. I preferred Jesus. It's been a success, I think. Lots of enthusiastic readers. I get countless emails and letters about it. My plan is to write two more books in the coming few years with some religious angle. I want to write a book on how to be a Christian, and I want to write a novel about Saint Paul.

LC: I read that you're in the process of writing a biography of Gore Vidal, to be published by Doubleday in 2015. As executor of his literary estate and a longtime friend for thirty years, as well as being an acclaimed biographer, you're the perfect person to write the book. But it does sound like an immense project, especially with Vidal's work branching into so many different areas. "The good biographer must find a mythos, or story, that will help to tame the myriad facts of the subject's life," you once wrote. Is there a particular aspect of his life and work, a story thread that you intend to focus on?

JP: I'm halfway through the Vidal book, which I've been (in a sense) writing for twenty-five years. I've got endless material. Endless. Some good stuff, mostly in the form of interviews with Gore and Howard (his partner) and various friends who knew Gore well over many years. I know this life well. It's a question of tone. That is evolving as I write. I may have to rewrite a lot of stuff. Some bits and pieces of this book were written in the early nineties, when I was planning to write a bio of Gore, but pulled back because I knew he'd be impossible about it.

LC: Over the years you've written many wonderful essays for *The Chronicle of Higher Education*. Some of the most fascinating ones were on authors like G.K. Chesterton, Henry James, and Rudyard Kipling. Your essay "Ruddy Good Show," where you write about attending a service of remembrance for Kipling, is a particularly good one. Kipling, you said, was one of your favorite writers and an underrated poet, and you've even visited his 17th-century manor house in east Sussex and his house in Brattleboro, Vermont, where he wrote *The Jungle Books*. Have you considered writing a full-length biography of him or any of these authors? Or will Vidal be your final biography for the time being?

JP: I won't ever write another conventional biography. I will, though, write more biographical fiction.

The Apprentice Lover
HarperCollins, 2002

LC: You've met and worked with some immensely significant writers, actors, and artists. Some you've told wonderful anecdotes about and some you've only mentioned in passing. One of those I'd love to learn more about is Graham Greene. You knew Greene personally, visiting him in Capri and, later, in Antibes toward the end of his life. You even wrote him into *The Apprentice Lover*, your sixth novel. What was Greene like as a person? I read an article by you where you talk about the books on his shelf, and it made me wonder if you talked about each other's writing. What did you learn about Greene from your conversations with him?

JP: I liked Greene very much. He was warm and seemed interested in what I was writing. I gave him one or two of my books. I didn't know him well, so it's hard to go into much detail. But there is a certain interest in meeting and talking with writers you admire. I liked meeting Borges, Neruda, Anthony Burgess, Auden, Anthony Powell, etc. Just to get a whiff of their presence.

LC: You've traveled widely over the last four decades and lived and worked in numerous countries. Wherever you've been, you seem to have always made the most of your time in a location. Even as a student in Scotland, you ended up meeting W.H. Auden on an excursion to Oxford. On an unintended night out in north London, you watched a lecture by Lord Melvyn Bragg that inspired you to write *Promised Land: Thirteen Books That Changed America*. While living in Italy, you ended up having dinner with Gore Vidal, who lived nearby—a stranger to you at the time. Do you have any regrets, Jay? Any occasions you've thought back on as missed opportunities? Perhaps a project or event you passed up on that you later wished you hadn't or a writer you could have met with but didn't?

JP: Well, I tried to make the most of being in a place. I was alert, looked around, wondered who might interest me. Do I have any regrets? I have endless regrets. They are mostly personal failings. Failures to be sympathetic enough or help someone. I dislike a lot of my own books, and wish I had done a better job on them. But I like a few as well. I suppose that life is like this. Generally, I feel as if that, given my limited talents—and I'm not being modest—I've managed well enough as a writer. I'm hoping to have a stretch of time ahead of me when I can write my best work. That's the plan!

LC: Tell us about your poem "Midrash," which is published in this anthology.

JP: The idea "Midrash" is that we're always—in a sense—creating commentaries, stories, examples, discourses on life. The original word goes back to the commentaries of teachers and Torah scholars in the period after the destruction of the Temple in Jerusalem. These commentaries were a way of getting in touch with the spirit of Judaism, of coming into the presence of the holy. I think of nature as a kind of holy text, and my own midrashic work is about getting in touch with the "wild abundance" all around. I start with that famous remark by Voltaire about the fact that we don't really have to conjure up God; he's already everywhere around us. And this from a man not considered by most to have an inkling of religious feeling! The poem is free verse, but I believe that no verse is really free. A good line of poetry expands to its right length, and moves onto the next line naturally.

Jay Parini's next collection of poetry, NEW AND COLLECTED POEMS, 1975-2015, will be published by Beacon Press in April 2016 and will include the poem "Midrash."

MIDRASH

Jay Parini

Voltaire once said
that all the arguments for God's existence
hardly add a thing to what
we know already, being here.
We've walked in corn rows in midsummer,
seen the field aflame.
Even in dank winter there was
light enough to satisfy our need
for reassurance. God is
everywhere in wild abundance.
He waves from terraces or even cries
from windows in the alley.
Wants us to believe in yellow beams
that fall across the floor,
the doughy light of mild mid-day,
the slough of afternoon's blue shade
or fireflies popping in the dusky hedges.
He would have us breathe slow breath.
And somewhere in the rooms of this big house,
he's singing without words
in brilliant passages
that find us even without looking.
Soon his grace-notes gladden us,
the humming mind within our mind.

THE SIBYL

John Mueter

Dr. Orion Westover, Ph.D., head of the Classics Department at Springfield University, eminent scholar, published author and gifted linguist, despite his middle-aged stodginess, was a man who loved adventure. Nothing pleased him more than to leave his cluttered office behind, hop on a plane, and get out "into the field" for the summer. He loved to poke about in the dusty stones of some ancient Greek or Roman ruins in order to decipher barely legible markings. Under the hot sun, the subject matter he studied so laboriously at his desk came to life and spoke to him.

Orion led a well-ordered life and saw himself as a rational and sensible man. Yet, in his deepest slumbers, when he had surrendered his normally obedient intellect to the alien regions of the dark, he frequently experienced the most remarkable dreams. They were vivid, disturbing, intoxicating, and they defied any kind of explanation or credence. His nocturnal visitors seemed to emerge from a realm nearly vanished in the haze of time. Warriors in glistening breastplates, frightening hags with bony hands, and laughing satyrs cavorting in olive groves inhabited these dreams. He suspected that even Athena and Apollo might have appeared to him. These exalted deities revealed wondrous things, revelations that he desperately tried to remember when he awoke—but they always dissipated like smoke from a chimney on a windy day. He didn't share these experiences with anyone, not even his adoring wife. His colleagues would have suspected that he had gone off the rails completely.

But one day, unexpectedly as the best things are, he made a

discovery that changed everything and put a new slant on the phenomenon of his nocturnal visions. In the Topeka Public Library, of all places, he came across an extraordinary book.

Stopping in Topeka had been a completely spontaneous decision. He was driving on the interstate, on his way west to a conference of Ancient Greek scholars in Colorado, when he decided to exit. He cruised through the downtown area in the hope to finding a suitable place to have lunch. Finding eateries that offered good quality food was always a challenge on these long road trips. He decided on a small café, where he consumed a passable tuna salad on rye. On his way out the door, he espied the public library just across the street, a handsome neoclassical edifice. It beckoned to him. It was his habit to check out the classics offerings of provincial collections. University bibliotheca were the most interesting, of course, but even municipal libraries could offer some pleasant surprises.

He browsed the small collection of books on classical subjects and was pleasantly surprised to find a few of the Loeb editions that offered original Greek or Latin texts with the translation on the opposing page. Not every library had those. He was ready to leave and head back to his car when, out of the corner of his eye, he noticed a volume on its side, behind the other books on that particular shelf. He carefully extricated the book from its hiding place. To his surprise, it was in German and by a scholar he had never come across before. The title was *Die Geheimnisse des sibyllinischen Mysteriums*, which translates as *Secrets of the Sibylline Mysteries*, by Eusebius Blankenschmidt. It had been published in Berlin in 1904. He was mightily intrigued as the subject of the Sibylline Oracles was a subject dear to his heart. The book didn't have a Topeka Library identifier in it. As there was no way he could check the book out—he didn't even live in Kansas—he did something he had never done before: he surreptitiously "borrowed" the book, concealing it under his tweed jacket while he headed for the exit. No alarms went off. If no one had even cracked the book open in over a century, who was going to miss it? He planned to send it back when he was done with it.

As he was quite fluent in German (not to mention Homeric Greek, Modern Greek, Latin, French, and Portuguese), he set to work translating his newly found treasure. It was a curious work, speaking with assured authority on subjects where most scholars tiptoed lightly. In chapter seven, entitled *The Enduring Presence of the Oracle*, he encountered a startling assertion: The Sibyl was still on this earth and accessible—if one knew how to find her. His heart was racing, his mouth dry like cotton balls as he read further. According to Blankenschmidt, the Sibyl, mouthpiece of the gods, still held court in Greece. And then the author gave the precise directions to the Oracle's whereabouts as well as the incantations needed to access her holy precinct. It was too preposterous! If he hadn't been reading this in a scholarly work, Orion would have dismissed it as some kind of hoax. Yet, the book was too old to be mere New Age claptrap, and its scholarly tone seemed authentic. He read on, enthralled. The prospect of meeting a living Sibyl filled him with an indescribable euphoria. He had to check it out.

Dr. Orion Westover had been to Greece dozens of times over the years. Although he wasn't planning on the trip just then, he decided to fly over as soon as the semester ended. After landing in Athens, and despite the fact that he was suffering from the effects of jet lag, he undertook the long and uncomfortable bus ride north to Delphi where he hoped to induce himself into a sibylline mood. He had visited the famous site many times before and knew it well. On his way up the hill to the site of what used to be the Oracle, he was, as on previous visits, saddened by the crass commercialism that blighted the place. There were trinket stalls and shops that sold tacky T-shirts. And then there were the hordes of people who traipsed up and down the hill. Where did they all come from?

What did they want? Of course, the Sibyl didn't reside in Dephi any more as the place was overrun with tourists. Her current abode, according to Blankenschmidt, was on the Aegean island of Samos, just off the coast of Asia Minor.

The following day, Orion sailed on the overnight ferry to Vathy, the main town on Samos. Upon disembarkation, he boarded a local bus that took him to the opposite end of the island. Beyond the last stop, the town of Karlovassi, there was forested, uninhabited mountainous terrain, a part of the island where even the locals rarely ventured. They believed that it was inhabited by ancient spirits.

Once a year, at the onset of spring, it was the custom of the old women of Karlovassi to process into the hills, carrying with them an idol festooned like the Virgin Mary. No one could say when this ritual had originated, it was so ancient. They reverently removed this relic from its shrine, located in one of the villages at the foot of the mountain, and ceremoniously carried it up the forest path, chanting all the way. A priest did not participate in this. The object of their veneration was, in fact, an ancient statue of the Goddess Demeter, dating from the third century BCE.

Orion took a room in Karlovassi's only hotel and rested up for the adventure that awaited him the next day. He could barely sleep for excitement. He got up early, checked his gear one last time, and set off. He had to hike uphill quite a few miles, but the walk was exhilarating. As he was an avid hiker, he was in good physical shape for the climb. He didn't encounter a single soul. The Aegean sun filtered through the lightly spaced pines, endowing the forest with an aura of timeless enchantment. Orion remembered that Pythagoras was born and had lived on the island of Samos, some 2,500 years ago. Perhaps, he mused, the ancient philosopher and mathematician had walked on this very path. It was an awe-inspiring thought.

He had Blankenschmidt's book with him, just to be on the

safe side, and had drawn himself a map according to the author's instructions. But after reaching the summit of the mountain and wandering about for a good hour, he realized that he was completely lost. He didn't know which way to turn. Then he saw it: the cleft in the rocks that Blankenschmidt described as the entry way to the Samian Oracle. It had been hidden behind a growth of trees. The space was really too small for an adult to slip into. The instructions demanded that one recite the correct incantations, close one's eyes, surrender to Apollo, and walk into the cleft. Despite the fact that it was too much like Harry Potter on platform nine and three-quarters at King's Cross Station, Orion summoned all the faith he could muster and—by Phoebus Apollo, son of Zeus!—it worked. He was in!

The passageway through the rock was still very narrow as well as unpleasantly dark and damp, but he forged on. After several minutes, he saw a bit of light ahead. He arrived at an open space in front of a cave. The place seemed to be deserted. He was amazed that he had managed to come this far, but now that he had reached the precinct of the Sibyl, he wasn't quite sure what to do next. He waited a few moments, then cleared his throat and began the lengthy salutation he had practiced, in Homeric Greek:

"O mighty Oracle, omniscient Sibyl, servant of Apollo, in your wisdom and mercy, hear my humble supplication for your attention..."

He continued on in this vein for a while. It seemed to do the trick as smoke began emanating from the cave itself. He could barely make out the figure of a woman, a very old one, shrouded in black, sitting on a tripod stool.

"Enough, you blithering fool!" came a penetrating screech from the cave. "Don't you think I know who you are and what you want?" Orion was stunned to hear this delivered in English, with the trace of a New Jersey accent. "I am the Oracle, the Seer, the Prophetess, am I not? And yes, I speak English, or any other lingo you care to use."

He switched to English himself. "Oh Revered Sibyl, hear my supplication."

"All right, already. You got my attention. Business first: where's your offering?"

Orion fished the jar of Samian honey he had purchased in Vathy out of his backpack and placed it on a low rock just in front of him.

"Good stuff, that. Now, what can I do for you?"

"Divine Sibyl, how is it that you are still functioning as the ancient oracle?" Orion's curiosity as to her continued existence superseded any questions he had about the future.

"As you well know, I am not divine. When Apollo granted my sisters and me a boon, we requested eternal life, but we neglected to ask for eternal youth to go with it. What a ferkakte deal that was! So we live on, just getting older." She stopped for a moment to cough vigorously. "This damn incense, just not used to it so much anymore. Believe me, you don't want to see me too clearly anyway. Helen of Troy I definitely ain't, ha-ha-ha!" She laughed heartily at her own joke. Orion was pleased to hear that she had a sense of humor.

"Anyway, there were ten of us. My sisters slumber on, but they will never die. I'm the only one still in business. Maybe the others are on a cruise of the Greek Islands, ha-ha-ha!"

The Sibyl's guffaws soon turned into a convulsion of hacking. When she had recovered she continued. "The Pythia in Delphi closed up shop a long time ago. It's terrible the way the place is overrun. You've seen it for yourself; so little reverence for the Mysteries." She shook her head and clicked her tongue. "This place is very difficult to find. Only the most dedicated, such as yourself, can succeed in locating me. And that is the way it should be. I have had a few visitors over the years. The last one was that German—what was his name?— Krankenblimp or something.

"It was Eusebius Blankenschmidt."

"That's right! My memory isn't what it used to be. See how you do when you're three thousand years old!

"But Blankenschmidt was here over a century ago!"

"A mere blink of the eye, as they say. He was very clever and was able to find me after much trial and error. He asked me if he could publish the secret of my location. I said sure, fine, no one will bother to come anyway. You see that I was right. Your finding that book, by the way, was no accident. The gods still work in the lives of those who pay attention to them."

Orion was really enjoying the conversation. It was not at all what he had imagined his meeting with the Sibyl would be like. He posed his next question: "What was it that really terminated the activity of the oracles?"

"Just don't get me started! That patriarchal, monotheistic fiddle-faddle of a religion--such a downer, so lacking in imagination, so heavy-handed, so booooooring! Where's the mystery? Where's the fun? Ugh!"

There was a long pause. Orion thought he should move on to another subject. He asked the first thing that popped into his head. "What does the future of humanity look like?"

"Future? You think you have a future? Ha! Look what you have done to the planet—you've ruined the place! In your endless greed and stupidity, you have raped Mother Earth. You just don't learn. In my day, humanity wasn't so smart either—they deforested nearly all of these beautiful islands. Men did that because they wanted the wood for their ships and they never thought of the consequences. That's the whole problem—you don't think things through! You just act, stupidly and blindly. There will be much turmoil in the future. Just don't ask me to give the specifics, because I won't. It wouldn't make a bit of difference anyway, even if I did. But just remember this, O mortal: no outside force is doing it to you—you have brought it on yourselves through your own actions. Humanity will survive. The mysteries will be restored. Men will again learn to revere Gaia, the Mother of the World." There was more coughing and sputtering, then a long silence. The Sibyl continued, "You must go now. I am getting tired."

Orion had many more questions, but it was clear that the audience with the Sibyl was over. He bowed deeply. "Thank you, Revered One, for receiving me."

As he turned to go, he heard one last bit of advice from the crone. "And you'd better get that incantation right or you'll be stuck here with me forever, ha-ha-ha!" The sound of her cackling echoed from the inside of the cave and receded to nothing.

Orion faced the far too-narrow cleft again and succeeded in passing through. He descended from the summit of the mountain as if he were walking on air. Who would believe that he had just had an interview with the living Sibyl of Samos? A few days later, he boarded his return flight to the States. There was nothing else in Greece that could top what he had just experienced.

Dr. Westover was inspired by his encounter on Samos and went on to write a book entitled The Oracle Speaks. Although he didn't directly describe his experience with the Sibyl, or the nature of his dreams, the passion and conviction with which he expressed himself raised eyebrows in academic circles. While he hinted that the Sibyl might still be a living presence, he didn't divulge too many details. The old crone should only be discovered by the truly perseverant, he reasoned. The introduction to his book included a hearty extension of thanks to Eusebius Blankenschmidt. His academic colleagues in the field of classical studies scratched their heads over the mention of that name.

The Public Library of Topeka received a curious package sometime later. It was a book, in German, along with a note from a Dr. Orion Westover of Springfield University, asking their pardon for making an unauthorized withdrawal of the material. The librarians were rather perplexed as the title of the book was not listed in their catalog, and they had never seen it before. It was added to the pile of unwanted books put aside for the next library sale. They were sure no one would ever buy it.

ANTIQUE ROSES

Robert Boucheron

At sunrise on a clear day in May, a silver-gray Explorer prowled the streets of Hapsburg, Virginia with the windows rolled down. A chorus of birds sang their hymn to dawn. The morning breeze wafted the scent of rose.

From a genuine damask, the driver thought.

He parked on a side street. Tall, gray-haired and bearded, heavier than his doctor would like, he emerged clad in khaki pants, fishing vest, and a porkpie hat. The fishing vest bristled with loops and pockets—for string, knives, clamps, pincers, small plastic bags, rolls of tape, vials, test tubes, and a spray water bottle. In a holster on his belt, he wore a pruning clipper.

He strode a shadowy lane, following his nose. He turned a corner to face a large, clapboard house, surely one of the best in town. A wrought-iron fence surrounded a magnificent garden. Lilac, hydrangea, pink cherry, snow-white crabapple, purple iris, red peony, blue columbine, and yellow daylily jostled for space.

Shrub roses climbed an arbor beyond. From the street, he suspected they were antique or heirloom roses, old stock from centuries ago, roses that scorned disease and drought to blossom year after year. They might blossom once or twice a season, but they were worth the wait and far more fragrant than modern hybrids. Some dedicated gardener had chosen them from a nursery catalog, paid dearly for them, and placed them in the right location. These roses were survivors.

Amid the multicolored splendor, a tall bush of dark green leaves foamed with white blooms. The flower looked to be double and cupped. Even from here, the perfume was strong.

Could it be a rose he had only read about, the sensation of Paris in 1832? The superintendent of the Luxembourg Gardens named it for his wife, "Madame Hardy." According to *The Old Shrub Roses*, by Graham Stuart Thomas:

> This rose, one of the most superlatively beautiful of the old white varieties, and having few peers among the colored varieties, is not a pure damask, but probably owes some of its beauty and vigor to *Rosa centifolia*. The clusters of flowers do, however, show this affinity, while the perfect shape of the blooms is found again only in some of the gallica roses. There is just a suspicion of flesh pink in the half-open buds, emerging from their long calyces, and the flowers open cupped, rapidly becoming flat, the outer petals reflexing, leaving the center almost concave of pure white, with a small green eye.

He pushed the gate. The rusty hinges shrieked. He padded up the walk and peered at the house. No sign of life in the windows, no lights or movement. He crossed a patch of grass, mowed and immaculate. The lower stems of the white rose were gnarled and brown, as thick as a forearm, with fearsome thorns. The upper stems were green and springy.

The blossoms at close range were lovelier than he imagined and abundant beyond belief. He plunged his face into a cluster of white and inhaled. The effect was like a drug. His heart raced, and his head floated. For this, he woke in the dark. For this, he forsook his warm bed to drive for miles on deserted country roads.

He glanced right and left. In the grip of emotion, he saw nothing. He heard nothing as he reached behind for the pruning clipper at his hip. He slipped the catch on the tool. He positioned the curved blade just below the junction of two stems. He squeezed.

Instead of a gentle snip, he heard the click of a gun safety catch. He raised his eyes. A few feet away, a rifle rested in the arms of an old woman in slippers and dressing gown, a woman with wrinkled cheeks and wild, white hair. Steely, blue eyes sighted along the barrel. Somewhere overhead, a mockingbird chose that moment to warble.

"Hold it right there, mister. Reach for the sky."

He complied, one hand holding the clipper and the other holding a rose.

"Caught you red-handed. Would you care to explain what you're doing on my property at this ungodly hour?"

He lowered his arms. The rifle wagged. The arms returned to a vertical position.

"Or do you expect me to guess?" She glanced up at the evidence suspended in midair.

"I generally ask permission, unless the house is uninhabited, or the specimen is in a graveyard or some public place. Your beautiful garden—clearly private—got the better of my judgment."

"Who are you?"

"Dr. Forest J. Blodgett, professor of botany."

"I should warn you, Dr. Blodgett, my vision is twenty-twenty. I have won first place for marksmanship at the Quidnunc County Fair more times than I can count. My finger is on the trigger."

"So it is, madam. Allow me to make amends."

"No need." She lowered the rifle and replaced the safety. "What's your game?"

"I collect old roses and propagate them. I'm a rose rustler. Do you happen to know the name of this specimen?"

"No. Do you?"

"I will need to do additional research. Provisionally, I would identify it as a variety from the nineteenth century. I hesitate to pronounce the name for fear of jinxing the identification. One of my superstitions."

"Hmph. Come inside and have breakfast."

She turned abruptly. He followed her to the back door and into the kitchen, a large, bare room with a massive stove.

"My name is Ella Eulalia Finch. Unmarried, so in formal situations I am called Miss Finch. This is not one of those situations. I was born and grew up in this house. My father was Judge Stephen Finch. From him, I inherited considerable real estate in town, rental property. I am active in the historical society."

She stood the rifle in a corner, next to a broom.

"Coffee?"

"Yes, please. Black." Forest sat at a plain pine table.

"Excellent choice. There's no milk in the house." She set a steaming mug before him.

"And the roses?" He slipped the pruner in its holster and placed the white rose on the table.

"Planted by my grandmother, Sadie. She was a woman of taste, if not of wealth. Family lore says that she scorned fine food and elaborate clothes. What she didn't spend on frippery she lavished on her home, including the garden. My mother helped tend it as a girl. To her it was a chore."

"And to you?"

"I preserve what's here. The roses are hardy. They tolerate wet and dry. A hard winter might freeze them back to the root. But those roots go deep. How do you like your eggs?"

"Over easy, thank you."

"Ham and biscuits from yesterday's baking. You know they're better the second day."

"Yes, indeed."

Ella Eulalia busied herself at the stove. Forest sipped his coffee. He knew better than to ask if he could help.

"Where are you from, family and so forth? In Virginia, we hardly know a person unless we know his ancestors, where they lived, and who they married. We may be cousins."

"I'm afraid my background will be a disappointment. I was adopted as an infant by Dr. James Blodgett and his wife, Lorena. He was a medical doctor, whereas I am a doctor of philosophy. They lived in Leesburg, where he had a general practice. After me, they adopted a baby girl, Renata. My sister and I grew up there and attended public school. She married and lives in New York. I continue to reside in Leesburg. Our parents are deceased, I regret to say."

Ella Eulalia set plates of ham and eggs on the table, a plate of biscuits warmed on the stove, a cut glass tray of butter, and a pot of jam.

"Put it up myself," she said. "Peaches from an orchard in the county."

"A woman of accomplishments."

"You're single, then? No children?"

"Correct."

"Adopted, you say. Any idea of your blood kin?"

"Back then, the information was secret. Agencies did not always keep good records, so it might be hard to trace today."

"I am familiar with official records."

"You said you were single?"

"Not quite. I said I was unmarried."

Forest chewed a mouthful of ham. He reached for another biscuit. He split it in half, applied butter to one half and jam to the other. He reunited the biscuit, now a sandwich, bit into it, and groaned with pleasure.

"I like to watch a man eat."

Forest raised his mug of coffee by way of a toast.

"After my mother died, I cooked for my father, here in this kitchen. Two older children had left home. I kept house, learned how to budget and how to shop. It was the dream of a certain strain of teenage girl to marry Father. In my case, the dream lasted until I was forty. That's when he died. Along the way, he taught me some legal jargon, how to research a deed in

154

the county courthouse, and how to manage property. He was the leading citizen of Hapsburg, a pillar of the church, and a sportsman. He hunted with the boys. Once a year, he took me duck hunting, just the two of us."

"A remarkable man."

Ella Eulalia finished what was on her plate, offered Forest more, and was pleased when he accepted another biscuit.

"Still," he said, "I don't see why you had to stay. If you had married and left home, your father could have hired a housekeeper."

"Since I am telling you, a complete stranger, the story of my life, I see no reason to hold back. When I was sixteen, I had a baby. In the 1950s, an unwed mother was shameful and an abortion was unthinkable. It was whispered that my mother died of grief. I wanted to marry the young man, but Father forbade it. He would not have a shiftless, penniless, no-account, goddamned Yankee for a son-in-law. It was the one occasion on which I heard him curse. Immediately after I gave birth, the baby was whisked away and put up for adoption. That's how it was in those days. Mother died of an enlarged thyroid, something that's treatable today. We were in shock. My reputation was ruined. I skipped the last year of high school. Later, Father reconsidered. By then, we had settled into a routine."

"An expiation."

"Come again?"

"A guilt offering." Forest swallowed the last of his coffee. "Was your baby a boy or girl?"

"A boy. What year were you born?"

"1955. What year was your baby born?"

"The same."

She studied her guest to see what he was thinking. She did not need to verify the face. She had made up her mind.

"Come with me."

She led him from the kitchen through a serving pantry, to a large dining room furnished with a table for eight and a matching sideboard. Facing west, the room was dim. She switched on the chandelier. Over the fireplace mantel hung an oil painting, a full-size portrait of a man dressed in a dark suit. The man was fair and erect, clean-shaven, with one hand placed on a leather-bound book, a law text.

"Stephen Finch in his prime," she said. "Except for the beard and the rustler getup, you could change places."

Forest stared at the portrait. Used to seeing his reflection in a mirror and his photograph in college publications, he did not see a resemblance. Stephen Finch on the wall was in his forties, florid and confident, while Forest Blodgett, in the flesh, was touched by age and disillusionment. How could he be the grandson of this man? How could this withered old woman be the girl who gave birth?

"How can I be your mother?" she asked.

"The timing is right, and the circumstances. The adoption agency placed babies close to where they were born, or so I was told. But my coming here today is sheer coincidence."

"Is it? When you search for antique roses, what are looking for?"

"Old rootstock, names, and lineage."

"Of the roses or those who planted them?"

"I have met some wonderful people in my quest, gardeners and botanists and people who love roses. You have a point."

"But no proof."

"Unless we submit to a DNA test," he said.

"I didn't think of that."

"Wait."

Forest fumbled with his vest, opened flaps, and dug into pockets. He produced a small object, a cheap signet ring. He held it between thumb and index finger. Ella Eulalia took it.

"Do you recognize it? It was given to my parents when they

156

got me, passed on by the agency. They said it was a keepsake."

Ella Eulalia gazed at the ring in the palm of her hand. The boss was engraved with a stylized rose. She spoke in a faraway voice.

"Howard bought it at Woolworth's as a gift. It was all he could afford, my engagement ring. We had a few days of happiness. Then he was driven out of town, almost tarred and feathered. I was upset, angry with Father. His word was law. The world was against me. I entrusted the ring with the child. It was a desperate gesture."

"But not impossible."

"No."

"Because here I am."

"My baby!"

Under the impartial gaze of the dead judge, mother and son embraced.

SURVIVAL OF THE FITTEST

Allister Timms

I used to entertain myself on wet and damp days in Wales by imagining my family as ants and trying to figure out how my mother would achieve a better social standing for us in the insect world. Would she push us to imitate bees or dragonflies? And I wondered how long the colony would tolerate us before they threw us out. We might be a bunch of unwanted worker ants, I could hear my mother saying, but there was a whole phylum of possibility waiting for us. And that's when the goldfinch would swoop in and snatch me away to a higher calling.

My mother immersed me into her ring of social refinement by demanding I attend choir practice, Scouts, piano lessons, Latin and Greek classes, classical topiary, Wall Street economics, Sunday School, church rumble sales, and equestrian lessons—which I fondly referred to as nag riding.

But her greatest *pièce de résistance* was elocution lessons. So it came as no surprise when, on the Saturday morning of my first lesson, my mother said, "If Margaret Thatcher can reclaim an island full of penguins, then by God, Queen, and Country, I'm going to make sure you learn how to rise above your social squatting position."

My only response to this was to crack my hard-boiled egg that nestled ever so gently in my Big Ears egg cup.

My mother sighed at the insurmountable task, but then must have remembered her Darwinian pledge because she snatched my hard-boiled egg and soldiers from under my nose, flung me into my coat, and drove me to my lesson.

To the best of my ability, I can't remember having diction

like Huckleberry Finn or a brogue that was so thick I could wear it on cold days but, nonetheless, it was decided by genetic vigor more vital than mine that I should have private elocution lessons.

We drove away in our recently purchased Renault 5, a jaunty French motor that cruised with cosmopolitan efficiency, but shifted with an audible grinding of gears. My mother turned on the radio, tapping her fingers on the steering wheel to some half-garbled pop song. I noticed how she avoided taking the motorway exit, but swung twice around the roundabout in order to clip along a country lane that led to an upmarket village. As coal miners walked out on strikes and clashed with police, my mother slowed for the posted speed limit, luxuriating in her surroundings as if in a bubble bath. She pointed out the enclave of tidy cottages now owned by the English. The spotless green sheen of the golf links. The straight telegraph poles. The commonplace boutique where bras supported well-endowed mannequins. The lack of tiresome sparrows and the abundance of swans gliding along the sluggish river.

"This is what the great naturalist intended," she sighed as the Renault spat out a dirty cloud behind us.

I wish I could have seen what my mother saw. My attention was focused on a stout basset hound trundling along the street, his testicles swinging back and forth. When he stopped at an empty kiosk, I knew what was coming. But, by then, my mother had floored the accelerator, her angry gaze fixed on the road ahead. Only once did she peek in the rearview mirror to make sure her unsullied village was still there.

*

My elocution teacher turned out to be an older woman from England. She was recently married and lived in an Edwardian house in a very urbane and self-selecting suburb of Llanelli called "Beagle End." She had a Volvo in the drive and ornamental cherry trees in the garden. Her husband was a younger man and a member of the local Conservative Party who had unsuccessfully tried to run on the ticket of slashing the unemployment benefit for the lazy and classless rabble that depended on the state like children. "Is this what Darwin had in mind when he wrote *On the Origin of Species*?" he'd asked rhetorically. Apparently, yes, because he lost the election in a landslide. But he'd won my mother's admiration, especially when she learned his wife was a speech teacher.

Mrs. Harding met my mother and me at the front door. She greeted us in a diction I'd only heard once before spoken by Steed from *The New Avengers*. She pronounced the simple "Hello" with all the blood of a century of aristocracy behind it. "Or should I say *Shw mae*?" she asked, sucking on the Welsh vowels like a boiled toffee. My mother was instantly impressed. Until Mrs. Harding opened the stained-glass door wider and my mother saw the dressing gown. There was a brief moment of hesitation. But then Mrs. Harding spoke again. "Won't you come in?" she said, making it sound so beguiling, so tempting, so completely alluring, that my mother melted like a young suitor before Greta Garbo. My mother shoved me in, said she'd pick me up in a half hour, glanced again at Mrs. Harding's dressing gown, shrugged, and left.

"This way, darling," said Mrs. Harding as the door shut with a well-pronounced click. I followed her into the room where she held her private lessons. It was furnished with soft, colorful linens, gossamer scarves, and hand-painted throws on the back of a leather couch and chair. A green and blue parrot hoisted his head feathers as I entered. There was a lush sheepskin laid out on the floor and fine silks draped over tall lamps. Potted ferns spread their large arms out in supplication and there were rich and sticky orchids heavy with scent in every nook and cranny.

"Have a seat, darling," Mrs. Harding said. It felt like a

velvet throw had enveloped me. I went weak at the knees and fell back into the lush leather couch.

"Get off that, you little shit!"

I shot up. Stared open-mouthed.

The parrot had spoken. It scowled at me from its dark, ageless eyes. Its head feathers sprang up like a row of knives, head bobbing back and forth as if it was having some kind of mental fit.

"Oh, Emerson, you naughty bird, you," sweet-talked Mrs. Harding. "Let's have none of that now."

"Fuck off," replied the bird.

Mrs. Harding sat in her chair as graceful as a gazelle and crossed her legs. "Take no notice of the parrot," she said to me. "It's having a bad day."

"Like hell," it replied, peeling a sunflower like a deranged madman.

"Shall we begin our lesson?" asked Mrs. Harding with a voice that could have made Cadbury try to figure out a way to sell it as a silky chocolate bar.

I felt myself dissolve into the leather seat. I would do anything this woman told me. Anything. "Yes," I sighed like a soft, down feather.

"Fat little twerp," laughed the parrot as a hail of sunflower seeds landed on my head.

"Emerson," scolded Mrs. Harding. "Will I have to cover you with the *Cloth*?"

"Pretty Polly. Who's a pretty Polly?"

"Good," said Mrs. Harding, prolonging it like a long string of honey. "Let's begin now, shall we?" She opened a book in her lap and handed it to me. "Please read me the first sentence."

I took the book like a devotee from a goddess.

Mrs. Harding flipped the lid off a silver box. Her long fingers removed a Turkish Delight and dusted the pink sweet into a mound of white powder.

I began to read: "Lady Sidwell stro... stroked her manservant's bulge as he shakily poured the tea. Her little Pekingese cocked its leg and peed on the manservant's polished shoes just as Lady Sidwell's husband, Lord Granthom Sidwell, walked into the dining room with his hunting gun cocked over his arm."

"Not bad," said Mrs. Harding. "Although we are going to have to work on that stutter. And we are going to have to do something with your diphthongs. And you're a bit too soft with consonants. Otherwise, not bad. Read on," she said with a wave of her hand as she settled back into her chair, the corners of her mouth dusted with white powder.

I coughed and flicked a few stray sunflower seeds from my lap. " 'What's for lunch?' snapped Lord Sidwell, a horde of yapping mutts in his wake. The manservant stared at the puddle around his feet as the silver ladle slipped into the soup tureen."

I would have read further if the parrot hadn't begun his antics again.

"Filthy harlot!" it screamed.

"Emerson! I will not take any more of your nonsense. Either you eat your seeds in peace, or I *will* use the Cloth."

The parrot hissed with its grayish tongue and grabbed another seed. He peeled it with his beak and mumbled something under his breath.

"I heard that," said Mrs. Harding.

I returned my attention to the book in my hand, *Lady Sidwell's Velvet Couch*, by Victoria Peacock. I swallowed hard and tried to concentrate on being less soft with my consonants and work on my diphthongs.

A sunflower shell landed on my head. Then another. Followed by two more.

"Read me some more," said Mrs. Harding, the exotic persuasion in her voice turning my head to soft, sifting sand.

I held the book before my face like it was a recently unearthed religious tablet full of wise words.

"When the manservant slowly swirled in the milk, Lady Sidwell squeezed her knees together. Her husband sat with a flatulent groan and eyed the soup tureen. 'Is there any roast beef?' He demanded. The manservant plopped two square sugar cubes into Lady Sidwell's delicate teacup as she kicked off her fluffy slippers under the table and wriggled her little toes."

"Much better that time," said Mrs. Harding. "The mellifluous tone of your Welsh accent played beautifully with the vowels. Go on, read me some more, there's a good boy. And this time, remember to breathe into the glottal stops and try not to sibilate too much."

I parroted in my head, *Anything you say…. Anything you say… Anything you say*.

I went to turn the page when Mr. Harding poked his head around the door. "My sweet Puss in Boots, would you have a minute to hear the speech I've written for the next party meeting?"

Mrs. Harding waved in my direction with sugar-dusted fingers. "I have a young student, darling," she said.

The parrot patrolled his perch and laughed like Rasputin.

"Apologies, my sweet dandelion." Mr. Harding squeezed his portly frame inside. "It's just you're so good at pointing out the bullshit."

The parrot cackled like a deranged bird of paradise.

"That noun," stressed Mrs. Harding "is not welcome in my sanctuary."

Mr. Harding hung his head and studied his scuffed wingtips.

"Fat twerp," shouted the parrot.

"Commie bastard," shouted Mr. Harding, his cheeks manifesting a violent scarlet.

"Enough," yelled Mrs. Harding. "Do you both want the Cloth?"

The parrot picked at its scaly feet. Mr. Harding picked at his bitten nails.

"Maybe I should come back later," said Mr. Harding.

"Yes, bugger off, fat lard," said the parrot, clasping and unclasping one clawed foot.

"Why, you filthy little hooligan," snarled Mr. Harding, lunging for the bird.

The parrot squawked and flapped its wings. "Go eat your onion rings, fatty," it chanted over and over.

Mr. Harding swiped at the parrot. "I'll murder you, you, ungrateful little foreigner."

I squeezed Victoria Peacock's book between my knocking knees, squishing my finger that bookmarked the page until it went numb and tingled.

"Spank me, darling," shouted the parrot.

"God will punish you for your insolence," roared Mr. Harding, his face as red as the devil's.

"That's it!" Mrs. Harding pushed aside her box of Turkish Delights and sprang out of her chair. Like a glamorous movie actress from the Roaring 20s, she slipped free of her gown and draped it over the parrot.

"You rotten bitch… You rotten bitch… You rotten bitch."

She grabbed her husband's wavy hair and dragged him out of the room as he spluttered and foamed. "I'll pluck that damn lazy bird and baste him with good English herbs."

Mrs. Harding slammed the door shut and, in the violent gust, a few petals fell from her delicate orchids.

The sound of Mr. Harding sobbing competed with the sibilant hisses from the parrot.

"He will stop that in a bit, darling," Mrs. Harding said to me as she slid back into her chair, dressed now only in a transparent nightdress. Her sugar-dusted fingers reached for another sweet. She lounged in her chair and nibbled on a Turkish Delight, sugary dust falling onto her diaphanous gown like fairy dust.

Emerson quit his racket.

Mr. Harding sobbed one last time and fell silent.

The shrill sound of the doorbell startled me.

"That will be your mother," said Mrs. Harding with a perfect sigh. "We shall have to stop for today." She rose from her seat and gently tugged her dressing gown off the parrot.

"You'll pay for that, you worthless slut," screeched Emerson.

"Shall we say the same time next week?" asked Mrs. Harding, stepping over Mr. Harding lying in a fetal position before her door.

"Yes," I replied with the best diction I could muster.

"Grand," said Mrs. Harding as she knotted her gown and brushed the sugar from her mouth.

My mother stood on the step in a glowing realm of excitement. "So, did he do well?" she asked.

"Perfect," purred Mrs. Harding. "Although he does need to work on his pronunciation. He has a tendency to rush his words together. But I'm quite sure I can help him with that."

"Oh, good," said my mother. "I was afraid he was a lost cause."

"Not yet," said Mrs. Harding, her sugar-dusted fingers beginning to close the door. "I'm of the opinion that my students should either excel or fail. In fact, I ascribe to the philosophy of survival of the fittest. Those who are willing to please me will succeed. Those who are not diligent with practice, I can do nothing for. It's all a matter of practice, perseverance, and taking pleasure with the English language. You either have it or you don't. And I would say that your boy could definitely have it."

The door was almost closed now. But before it did, a sultry "Goodbye," drifted out of Mrs. Harding's house like a kiss.

"You see," said my mother as we drove home, "if a person puts their mind to something, they can do it. They can change.

That's what Mr. Darwin was on about. Change or meet the Dodo."

"I know," I said, "even her parrot speaks."

A triumphant smile crossed my mother's face. "Her parrot speaks! Imagine what she can do for you, then."

THE HILL BEHIND THE HOUSE

Michael C. Keith

Since he'd been a toddler, twelve-year-old Haley Morgan feared what was on the other side of the rocky hill that rose to the west of his family's ranch. Even when he played, he would not go beyond a certain point, afraid that he might be seen by whatever evil he was sure lurked beyond. On horseback rides, he steered clear of the narrow trails that led behind Clifford Butte.

"Why's that old hill called Clifford Butte, Mom? Our land goes all the way to it, right? Shouldn't it be *Morgan* Butte?" Haley had asked, years earlier.

"It was called that long before your grandpa bought the ranch, honey. Bet almost a hundred years back. Maybe more."

"Well, who was Clifford Butte?"

"Just Clifford, sweetie. Butte is another word for hill. I'm not sure who Clifford was."

"Maybe Daddy knows. Bet Grandpa would . . . if he was still alive."

"I don't think your dad knows, but it wouldn't hurt to ask him, Haley."

To Haley's disappointment, his father couldn't tell him much about the hill behind the house either. Only that Clifford was probably a pioneer homesteader who had put his handle on it.

"When people first came out here from the East, they stuck names on everything. Guess it made 'em feel like they belonged. Kind of like animals that spray on things to make them their own."

*

Haley's initial curiosity about the hill had turned into trepidation when he came to regard its moonlight silhouette as a giant head emerging from the dusty plains. His imagination quickly conferred grotesque characteristics on it, including a set of devilish horns. A series of unusual sightings over the next handful of years convinced him that the jagged skull-like mound at the far reaches of his backyard concealed awful secrets.

Among the many things that intensified his dread was the roar of thunder and flashes of lightning that came from its direction, especially on summer evenings. Haley had also witnessed large birds—hawks—hovering over the hill's peak, only to vanish on its far side. Once he saw a plane disappear behind the rise as it streaked across the cloudless sky. He had waited with growing anxiety for it to emerge on the butte's south side . . . but it never did. *How could that be? Did something grab it?* he wondered.

Then there were the countless stars that fell to earth behind the monster's head and the sudden bright glows that followed. Some nights Haley lost count of how many there were, and it seemed to him like some horrible force was sucking up the heavens. When he talked about this with his parents, they assured him the world was not coming to an end as he feared.

"What's in back of the hill, Mom?" Haley had asked numerous times.

"Just more of what's in front of it, I suppose. Nothing back there that I know of. No roads go behind it. You should take a ride out there with your daddy and see for yourself."

Haley mulled over the idea and eventually mustered the courage to propose the idea to his father, who agreed to take a horseback trip around the base of the butte. But days became weeks and then months and no such expedition took place. *Who cares what's back there?* thought Haley in frustration, though his curiosity over Clifford Butte's hidden side continued to deepen.

Haley could see the hill from his bed, and on most nights it was the last thing he saw before going to sleep. His dreams were filled with haunting images of the hidden world that lay behind the bluff, and he was always an unwilling part of them. Invariably they would end with him running away, pursued by something terrible that was out to seize him.

*

The morning following his twelfth birthday, Haley rose from his bed determined once and for all to see for himself what lay behind the hill . . . to demystify it. He saddled his horse and set out on his mission.

"C'mon, Kelly, you can come with us to that old dumb hill," shouted Haley to his dog. "Bark if you see something, okay?"

As Clifford Butte drew closer, Haley's resolve waned and then vanished completely when he heard a crack of thunder up ahead.

He turned his horse and called to Kelly. "We better get back home in case that storm gets to this side of the butte."

Within minutes he was back on his front porch waiting for the storm to move beyond the butte, but as usual it never did. The next morning he was suddenly awakened as Kelly leapt from his bed and dashed out of the room. It was as if the dog was responding to a command, yet Haley had heard no voice. He went to his window and saw the retriever running toward Clifford Butte.

"No, no, don't go there, Kelly," he mumbled, quickly removing his pajamas and throwing on his jeans and t-shirt.

"Where do you think you're going, Mister?" asked Sheila Morgan, blocking her son's path to the front door.

"I've got to get Kelly," he answered, breathlessly.

"Not before you have your breakfast. And where is Kelly going that's so important you have to go after him?"

"Out to Clifford Butte."

"So, what's the matter with that? He wanders all over the territory every day."

"But he's going to the other side, Ma."

"Why would he go there rather than any other place? What's the big deal?"

"But, Mom . . ."

"Look, eat your cereal and do your chores. Then you can go after him."

*

Too anxious to really eat, Haley nibbled at his breakfast enough to placate his mother and then headed out to locate his best friend. Kelly had been a part of his life for as long as he could remember, and if it hadn't been for him, Haley would not have had anyone to play with, since the Morgans' closest neighbors with kids his age were a dozen miles away.

Haley saddled up and galloped toward the looming object. For the first time ever, he rode around the side of the outcropping.

"Kelly," he called softly, his heart racing.

He raised the volume of his voice as he rode deeper into the hill's unknown landscape. When he reached what he calculated to be the dead center of the butte's far side, he heard a whimper and spotted his dog. To Haley's astonishment, Kelly was suspended in air. He slowly revolved while looking upward at the empty sky. A high pitch sound caused Haley to cover his ears. He climbed down from his horse and inched toward the dog, which hung at eye level with him.

"It's all right, Kelly," mumbled Haley, horrified by the bizarre sight before him. "What are you looking at, boy? There's nothing up there."

As soon as Haley made physical contact with the dog, Kelly dropped to the ground. The abrupt movement prompted Haley to do the same. Both he and his dog remained motionless on the parched terrain for several minutes until it felt safe enough to stand.

"Let's go home, Kelly," whispered Haley, moving toward his horse. In three quarters of an hour, they were back at the Morgans' ranch.

*

"Made it in time for lunch, I see. And you found Kelly. I saw you coming from the side of Clifford Butte. Did you finally discover what's behind it?" asked his mother.

" Yeah . . ."

"Well, so what's back there, honey?"

"Nothing. Same as in front of it . . . like you said. Just open space," answered Haley, deciding to say nothing about what he'd actually seen.

For some inexplicable reason, something in him suggested that whatever existed out there

was better left unrevealed.

"That's what I figured. More endless country. Just goes on forever. We got it out here in spades. Go sit on the porch with Kelly, and I'll bring you a sandwich."

For the rest of the afternoon, Haley gazed intently at Clifford Butte. Finally, he stood up and nodded in its direction.

The sun had set when Haley's mother realized he was nowhere to be found. Both she and her husband checked all areas of the ranch and then found that their son's horse was gone.

"I haven't seen Kelly either," said Mrs. Morgan, growing frantic.

"Well, where the heck could he be?"

"Maybe he went back . . ."

"Back where?"

Sheila pointed in the direction of Clifford Butte. "He was

there earlier today looking for Kelly."

"But why would he go back this late?"

It was at that moment that the sky lit up behind the butte. The Morgans shielded their eyes from the intense glare and were nearly knocked off their feet by a sudden blast of wind from the west. As quickly as this happened, calm returned.

"Oh, my God. What was that?"

"I'll call the sheriff," said Mr. Morgan, rushing into the house.

While Haley's horse and dog were eventually found in the next county, the search for him was officially called off after two weeks. The authorities declared him a missing person and circulated flyers with his picture throughout the state.

Unwilling to accept the fate of her son, Sheila Morgan made daily visits to Clifford Butte for the next twenty years until she was incapacitated by late stage cancer. In the final hours of her life, her child, unchanged by the passing of time, returned to her side.

"Where did you go, Haley?" asked Sheila, clutching his hand.

"Everywhere, Mom. I've been *everywhere.*"

ENTER THE TRAVELLERS

Joe Mills

Twice, Shakespeare took off,
disappearing from the grid.
The "lost years" they're called
by scholars although he knew
where he was. Maybe it was surfing
in Costa Rica or climbing in Tibet,
but more likely he sailed
into Boston or Savannah,
then started hitchhiking West.
He talked and drank and smoked
with whomever he met.
Lewis and Clark. Kerouac.
Custer. Crazy Horse.
He hung out for a while
with other ex-pats in Hollywood
then headed North to the Bay area
where he sat in with The Warlocks,
Jerry teaching him bar chords
in exchange for hearing madrigals.
Dylan mentions it in *Blonde on Blonde*,
but that's not good enough
for academics. They want to find
buried somewhere in an archives
a receipt for the pink Cadillac he rented
to drive Route 66. The initials WS
scratched in places on a waiver.
But they won't. In those years,
wherever he was,
he was just trucking,
keeping a low profile,
and not writing a thing,
not even a postcard to Anne.

SEGWAY WITH THE BULLS

Geoffrey B. Cain

Robert woke up and was not sure where he was. He could hear Susan breathing gently next to him but the surroundings did not tell him where he was. It is not that they were unfamiliar. No, they were too familiar. The same clean lines, muted tones, wood veneers, low and efficient, clean, and economical. The same Danish modern look throughout the Greyline Hotel chain whether you are in Istanbul or Jerusalem, Rome or Paris, London or Copenhagen. And Robert generally liked it that way. He knew how to work the cleverly recessed light panels and fixtures. He knew exactly where his clothes would go and how much room he had in the shower. Despite the fact that he thought the rooms were a little too small, a little too cold, and a little too efficient he at least knew what he was getting. There was a certain comfort in the uniformity and the newness that reminded him of everything that was the best of home. Outside of the hotel, he was sure the streets teemed with the desperate and the poor, taxi cabs belching leaded gasoline, aggressive vendors, angry police, impatient waiters, tour guides, other tourists, stalls of unrefrigerated food, the ancient greasy black walls of unrenovated buildings, and unchecked urban decay left intact through some misguided sense of history. But inside the hotel, he knew his room waited with its tiny, lukewarm shower, and a faint low-pitched hum from a transformer burning out in a low-watt, eco-friendly light bulb that almost gives just enough light. And another faint, barely audible, even lower pitched hum that comes through the vents from the compressor used to drive the thermodynamic refrigeration cycle of the building's HVAC system. Robert used to design such systems before he retired early. Such sounds were music to his ears that lulled him to sleep.

The light that came through the window gave no clue to where he was. He ruled out London. Surely they were in Brussels by now. Susan wanted to tour the great art museums and do some wine tasting on the Mediterranean coast. He thought that all of the really great art in Europe was already acquired by the various American robber barons of the last century. One can see them in the National Gallery, New York, or Chicago. How can any bowl of fruit in France be better than the one's that were acquired by art experts years ago? But Susan was passionate about these trips, and he knew enough not to say this out loud. He accepted that someone like Susan, with her humanities degree and her love of the arts, complemented a man like himself, an engineer with a mathematical mind.

He thought about dinner last night. It was the Dulce Carne de Giocomina. It was what he always ordered abroad. The Greyline Hotels always served it but sometimes with local variations. That is what made it interesting. It generally consisted of breaded and fried chunks of pork in a sweet pepper sauce over pasta, usually rigatoni. In Rome, it was garnished with capers and pecorino romano. In Amsterdam, it was a cream sauce and topped with a poached egg. In Austria or Switzerland (he couldn't remember which) it was topped with melted cheese and some kind of ham. He thought about last night's meal and it drew a blank. There wasn't a cheese course, there wasn't a recommended wine, and it was nearly the same as Rome, Florence, and Austria. "Where are we?" he thought.

"We have to get there really early," said Susan, rolling over. "What time is it?" The red LEDs on the clock radio read 5:30 a.m. "Come on we will be late." It was getting more and more difficult for Robert to get up - he had a sedentary job and never really bothered to exercise until he had retired: he was not in good shape and had bad knees. The travel and all of the walking around took a lot out of him. Susan was in the same boat though, just more enthusiastic.

"Where are we going first?" he asked, hoping to get a clue as to where they were.

"We will grab a coffee and a roll or something in the lobby," she said, "we meet the others in the lobby, we will head down to the rental place to meet the other guide, and we will be just in time for the bulls."

Spain, he thought; we are in Spain. Susan had always wanted to go to Spain. It had been all worked out.

They were in Pamplona for the festival of San Fermin. They were there as part of a package deal: hotel, Bull Run, and premium tickets at the bullfight. They were met by others who were also there for the package deal. They were all dressed in the white T-shirts with the faux red cummerbund painted on them and the tour leader was handing out the traditional red neck scarves.

"I am not sure if I can do this," said Robert. "My knees are no good. I feel like I am just asking for it."

"Don't be ridiculous," she said with a frown, "its all been planned. It will be exhilarating. And besides, we have gone over all of this before. It is perfectly safe. There are 98% less casualties than running the bulls the old way. It will be fun."

Robert thought that there was something strange about how she said that. Somewhere beneath the eons of layers of the yellow dust of the streets of Pamplona was a thin red sacrificial layer of 98% less casualties.

It was going to be a hot day today. He could tell. It was early and yet the sun already felt like it was beating down. He began to sweat.

But she was right, he probably could do this. He had already ridden a Segway on the Champs Elysee in Paris. The local tourist board successfully lobbied the city to pave over some of the cobblestones with asphalt to make way for the innovation. He had ridden Segways in Berlin and through Red Square in Moscow. He knew how to do this. He just wanted to keep up. They were to get on the Segways and travel down a special corridor next to the street that had been especially created for them. But there were just too many people. Masses of young men holding one another and praying. Masses of young virile men chanting. There were masses of young men already drunk. The dust began to rise as the police marched forward and the first rocket was fired down the street. A young child was selling leathery triangles of what might have been horsehide as "bulls' ears." The corridor would make it safe. He had seen the drawings in the brochure. It had been all worked out.

He stood tall in the Segway. A brass band began to play; randomly at first but slowly they mustered themselves into a rhythmic tune of some sort that apparently required no particular key to be agreed upon. A fight was breaking out down the street and three policemen ran towards the dusty circle of spectators.

Some of the young men had not been around Segways before and seemed nervous. They seemed fitful and easily startled. Suddenly, a small group lurched forward in the stray blast of a coronet and the firing of the rocket. Robert fell forward and the Segway followed the young men down the street. The size of the bulls sent a shock through Robert. The other Segways peeled off into their corridor as the bulls made their way down the street. Their guide's safely behind them and the gate of the corridor protecting them from harm. Robert was impressed that the young men could run so much faster than him. The locals waved their hats and screamed. He thought that they were very emotional. He turned around to see where the other Segways and Susan were and then he saw them coming: three large bulls, running up the street, their hooves exploding in the dust. He leaned forward to go faster and accidentally knocked down one of the young men. Other young men jumped out of the way of the machine, swearing at the top of their lungs. Some of the young men accidently ran into the corridor and were now running for their lives in front of the Segways. Their pilots did not see the young men but were transfixed by the bulls that ran next to them. A scream shot up through the crowd as Susan recognized Robert on the Segway ahead of the bulls.

It all happened so fast. The wheel of Robert's Segway was clipped by the heel of a bull and sent him careening into the corridor gate and into the waiting arms of an ambulance attendant. One unfortunate young man, who had drunk a considerable amount of wine that morning and the previous night, was hit by a Segway rider and sent to the hospital with a broken leg. Two other runners were gored after Robert's Segway impeded their run across the square.

Robert didn't mind the hospital so much. Once he got over the fear of foreign medicine, he began to appreciate the appointments of a Spanish hospital room. The faucet never really turns off, the light is not quite bright enough, the bed is just a little bit too short, the blankets just a little too thin, and there is not really enough room, but there was something about the place that made him feel at home. It was a small room. The doctors and the nurses always seem to be walking over one another. But fortunately the food is much better. And to his surprise, for dinner, there was Carne Dulce de Giacomina.

THE HIGH COLONIC
Raymond Abbott

Some years ago I bought a four-volume boxed set of hardcover books published by Harvard University Press. The books were on a remaindered table; they were cheap and were purported to be the condensed version of thirty-two years' worth of diaries written by an eccentric in Boston. The fellow was originally from Georgia, and he may have been independently wealthy, or if not exactly so, sufficiently well-off to keep him from having to work for a living. As my title suggests, this man believed in the health benefits of the High Colonic, popular in the 'Thirties (and before then, I am sure), which essentially lauds the value of the daily cleansing of the colon by enema, using large amounts of water and going high up into the colon.

Other practices that he adhered to included hiring persons from the community to read to him, often each day. I suppose it was books, but also newspapers and magazines, certainly, and he made notes, recording his thoughts about what was read to him. I found his writing quite absorbing, interesting and well-written, and so I read all four of the volumes. I can hardly begin to tell you, the reader, all that he had to say, but for purposes of this narrative, I will mention one event that sticks in my mind. And it was this.

He was married (although later, his high colonic doctor ran off with his wife) and he had the belief that women were most assuredly the weaker sex, and that applied definitely and specifically to his wife. Women were not tough enough, too puny ('puny' is my word, however.) As a remedy for this weakness, he believed he must beat his wife daily, beat her in the shins, with a thick, old-fashioned Coke bottle, the kind no longer seen today. It never sounded to me like an appropriate thing to do, and his wife apparently did not appreciate his efforts, but for some reason, she tolerated his behavior for some time, for he banged on her shins for years. I always remembered this abuse above all else from this man's extensive writings.

Years later I was to spend a few weeks at the MacDowell Colony in New Hampshire. It is a retreat for artists and for writers such as myself. When I was younger, I was invited there several times, but today I don't think I could get in, what with the great number of writers seeking admission now. I feel certain this is true, because the last time I applied, I was turned away.

It was at one of my MacDowell stays that I got to know a woman who wrote historical fiction. She was quite successful in getting her books published. I was about thirty at the time, and I suspect she was crowding sixty. I would say her name was Marian, but it could have been Mary, not that it matters to what I have to say.

There were several round tables in the dining hall at MacDowell, with half a dozen or more persons seated at each table. Three tables were set up for dining, and during my four-week stay, I sat at a table with Marian (or Mary) more than once. She was blonde, but could have been wearing a wig; she had a round, fleshy face, to which she applied heavy make-up and bright-red lipstick. It was a friendly face, though, and she laughed a lot and often had quite a bit to say. She had numerous good stories to relate, but I only remember one now, which I shall soon tell.

There was no particular seating assignment at these tables. A person could sit wherever he or she wished, but most evenings, the tables were full, which meant about fifteen were at MacDowell at the time I was there. Marian would often arrive a little late, making her entrance with a bit of a flourish. She usually was dressed in a silky, loose-fitting caftan of some sort, which I have noticed is commonly worn by women who are on the stout side. To me, what she wore looked like bedtime attire, but I suppose it was not. Often, her garments were quite colorful.

I paid no particular attention to Marian, although we spoke occasionally when we'd meet on the grounds. This particular night I am remembering began like any other, with the conversation light and breezy. As the diners at our table finished their meals, they got up to leave, until it was just Marian and I left. I was sipping my decaf coffee—I don't sleep well, didn't, even then—and I am uncertain how a suddenly serious conversation began, but it surely did.

She said, "Ray, you know I had one child, a girl." I guessed, and correctly so, by the way she spoke of her, that she was no longer with us. "She was an adventuresome sort, simply brave to a fault. If she had been a journalist today, she would have volunteered for the hotspots of the world." She never told me what her daughter did for a living, if anything. Or her name. She continued.

"I mean, she climbed mountains, she went deep-sea diving. Anything adventuresome or risky, she was there. I encouraged her, too." She paused as if she was unsure if she wanted to go on. I noticed that her face, ordinarily lively, was sad and tired-looking now. "She was living in London and got involved somehow in ferrying a cabin cruiser of some sort across the English Channel to France, not a terribly long distance, but that stretch of water can be treacherous, and it became just that. And soon after they left, or so I am told. She was the only woman on board, just past thirty years old, and in the company of six men." I was beginning to realize she had told this story before, though perhaps not often. I don't know why I came to that conclusion. She paused again as she seemed to need to compose herself somewhat.

"The craft sank in the rough seas," she continued, "and my

daughter perished, but the six men all survived." She said this with no rancor I could detect, but she must have wondered if her daughter was somehow abandoned. How could she not wonder? "You know, Ray, the biggest regret in my life is that I was so encouraging of her risk-taking. I was a fool! I regret that more than anything else. And more so each day."

I figured that was the moral of the story, suggesting to me, that if I had children, that I not make the same mistake she made (later in my life I did have one daughter).

Good advice, good message, of course. Solid.

I felt I needed to say something in reply, and somehow the story of the Coke bottle popped into my mind. And so I told Marian about the eccentric individual from Boston, by way of Georgia, and how he pounded his wife's shins with the soda bottle almost daily to toughen her up for life. And then I found myself saying to her, in great seriousness, that if her daughter had undergone the toughening up with the Coke bottle I spoke of, might she have somehow survived, perhaps?

Marian laughed a weak, confused laugh at the absurdity of what I was saying. The pure ridiculousness of my thinking, I suppose, struck her, but she replied, "I guess," and quietly excused herself, saying no more.

I noticed at future dinners—for I had two more weeks at MacDowell—Marian always sat at the most distant table from where I was sitting. I really didn't then understand why, although from today's perspective, at age seventy, I can better appreciate her aversion to me. Sometimes, though, I would catch her looking in my direction during dinner, but she avoided meeting my gaze, and we never again had a conversation. Not so much as a 'hello' in passing.

A CONVERSATION WITH SCOTT DOMINIC CARPENTER

Lowestoft Chronicle, November 2014

Scott Dominic Carpenter
(Photography: Paul Carpenter)

In 2013, Scott Dominic Carpenter, a professor of French literature and literary theory, best known for his scholarly books on nineteenth-century French literature and culture, made his literary debut with the short story collection *This Jealous Earth*. Months after the book was featured on Minnesota Public Radio and praised by *Publishers Weekly* as "engaging throughout," his debut novel, *Theory of Remainders*, hit the bookstands to a ballyhoo of critical plaudits. Among the many tributes the novel garnered were starred reviews from the *Library Journal* and *Kirkus Review*, the latter describing it as "a stellar achievement." The book went on to become a Midwest Connections "Pick" by the Midwest Independent Bookseller's Association and was selected for the esteemed *Kirkus Reviews*' "Best Books of 2013" list.

Earlier this month, *Lowestoft Chronicle* spoke to Scott Dominic Carpenter about his tour-de-force novel, his impressive debut story collection, and his latest published piece of creative writing.

Theory of Remainders
Winter Goose Publishing, 2013

Lowestoft Chronicle (LC): Scott, I thought your novel *Theory of Remainders* was outstanding—ingenious, insightful and riveting from the first page to the last. It's become one of my absolute favorite books. It's not just the story or the fully-rounded characters that make it so compelling, it's also the elegance of the prose and your profound exploration of language. In much the same way as your protagonist, Dr. Philip Adler, probes his patient's words for hidden meanings and stalks the town of Yvetot, searching for buried secrets relating to his missing daughter, you seem to have a compulsive interest in linguistics. Is that acute interest in language something that comes naturally, or something you made a deliberate effort to focus on for this novel?

Scott Dominic Carpenter (SDC): First of all, thanks for the kind words. Each time a reader connects with the book, I get a little thrill.

Regarding the linguistic turn of *Theory of Remainders*, much of it comes from me. The easy answer is that I teach French literature, do work in Spanish and German, and splash about in a few other languages. These interests certainly spill into the book. But where does this passion come from? I'm fascinated by the role of ambiguity—by the way language both reveals and conceals meaning. Everything we say drips with hints and secrets. This novel gave me a chance to express my understanding of language concretely and dramatically.

LC: How did the idea for *Theory of Remainders* come about? Was it something you began while you were living in Normandy?

The idea of WW2 relics (remainders) like unexploded bombs belatedly rising to the surface to cause further damage underpins the story. Did your research into places like Rouen and Yvetot and the German occupation of that region during WW2 influence the plot?

SDC: It's hard for me to pinpoint "the" idea for the novel, as if there were some original kernel. Different threads have different histories. It's true that I've lived in France for quite a number of years, and the environment of Normandy is especially suitable for the story—in part because it's a privileged site of French-American interaction (because of D-Day, etc.). And yes, I did a lot of documentation in the towns of Yvetot and Rouen, taking scads of photographs to help me convey a sense of place. But part of the story comes from my experience in Minnesota, where I moved in 1990. Just before my arrival, a young boy, Jacob Wetterling, was abducted and never recovered. To this day the family and authorities continue to search for him, and I was struck by what it must be like for the parents to live with that lack of closure. When things are left over like that—when there are such "remainders"—it's tough to live with.

LC: Incidentally, am I right in thinking the novel is set in 2008? Is that when you started writing the book, or did you choose that date for another reason?

SDC: That's right: the "present" of the book is set in 2008, though the traumatic events that motivate Philip Adler took place some fifteen years earlier. The specific dates are not significant, but I did want to keep it contemporary while dividing it between the present and the past. Since 2001 (roughly the midpoint between the two "times" of my novel) we've all been living in a world fraught with trauma of many sorts, and although the novel doesn't invoke any geopolitical events, this sense of loss was present as I imagined the tale. And yes, I did start working on it around 2008.

LC: Some authors work off a detailed plot outline, while others say they don't outline at all. What was your process for writing *Theory of Remainders*? And was it written from beginning to end, or in parts?

SDC: The writing itself was an adventure. This is my first novel, so I had a lot of false starts. I did outline the story, but only in rough terms. (I find that it's not fruitful to go into too much detail, for I may find my characters don't want to toe the line of my plot. Above all, you must remain faithful to the psychology of your characters.) The important thing is that I had a clear vision of the ending I wanted, and that gave me a clear sense of direction, a destination. Most of the writing followed the chronology of events, but there were many deep rewrites, during which I eliminated or created characters, or restructured significant elements. For example, the character of Melanie, who comes up in the first scene, was originally quite minor; in the final version she plays an integral role throughout the novel.

LC: Initially, I was slightly surprised by Dr. Adler continuing his therapy sessions with Melanie by phone while he was overseas. I wondered if it was normal practice in psychiatry. However, you made a strong case for why it was necessary— for Adler as much as Melanie. In the end, I thought it was an inspired decision to make her one of the main characters. Was it feedback from others that prompted the deep rewrites or did you make that decision yourself?

SDC: Well, there's a surprise there, too. As you know, Philip Adler is falling apart at the seams—almost literally—so he's engaging in some unconventional practices. When I hit upon the idea of the phone sessions, I considered it to be another sign of this deterioration. But then I learned from a reader (a psychiatrist) that such sessions are sometimes done. In fact, I've had a number of psychiatrists and psychologists tell me how authentic my portrayal of talk therapy is. I guess the research paid off.

LC: There's a wonderfully amusing opening to the book where one of Dr. Adler's sessions gets out of hand, resulting in his patient hurling objects at him. "A flapping mass with gray-white wings careened over his head, smacked into the wall, and collapsed. He swiveled around to examine the corpse. It was the book from the end table."

There are some other equally humorous moments in the book, and just as delightfully worded. As someone with a strong propensity for humor (a perfect example of it can be found in the exceedingly funny story "Sincerely Yours" from your story collection *This Jealous Earth*), what made you want to write a mystery novel, especially one with such a grim subject matter? After all, at the heart of the novel is the story of a father reliving the trauma of fifteen years earlier by investigating the murder of his only daughter.

SDC: I'm so glad you asked. It's true that I have a deep appreciation for humor. At the same time, I'm drawn to tragic and poignant events. I've always been struck by how life slaps the modes of tragedy and comedy together: you can be watching an aged parent die in a hospital bed, and at the same time, through the glass door of the room, you see an orderly pick his nose and study the prize at the tip of his finger. The grotesque never steps aside to allow the sublime to pass. Instead, it puts out its foot to trip it up.

I remember the evening before my own father's funeral,

when my siblings and I sat around and swapped stories. We quickly devolved into hilarity, even at this sober moment. It's not disrespectful; humor is sometimes the only way we have to make the horrid bearable.

LC: The scenes between Dr. Adler and the disturbed psychiatric patient Édouard Morin are extraordinary and totally unexpected. Did you always have in mind that Morin would be this eccentric, erudite, arcane character, or did he change as the novel progressed?

SDC: Morin is probably my favorite character. In some ways he is like Philip Adler, but in an exaggerated and monstrous way. Yet he is also a tortured soul, which makes him interesting at the same time he's repulsive. I latched onto the character of Édouard Morin very early on in the process—even before I had a good idea of who Philip Adler would be. He represents all that is impenetrable and obscure in language—all that language cannot say.

LC: Your short story collection *This Jealous Earth* comprises

This Jealous Earth
MG Press, 2013

sixteen tales, many of which were published in magazines between 2007 and 2012. Some are short pieces of less than 500 words, while others exceed 5,000 words. As for a unifying theme, "the stories are bound together by the question of choice: in each story characters arrive at a fork in the road, and they need to choose a path that will alter their future in important ways." Was it an obvious choice which ones to include? Am I right in thinking that stories like "The

Painting Boy" (where the boy has already made his choice), "The Parasite," and "Thursday," were discarded because they didn't fit with the others? And did you ever consider fleshing out any of the shorter pieces or reworking stories that didn't make the cut?

SDC: Actually, it was a huge challenge to figure out which stories to include. I hated to cut any. But some were discarded because of thematic difference (as you suggest, because the story didn't hinge on a choice), and some because of tone or genre. (For instance, "The Parasite" is a kind of short fable.) But then, in the second edition of the book we included a short piece at the end called "The Bait"—which is a kind of small gift to the reader, free of choice, rather charming, and not entirely consistent with the themes. And yet it felt right. So, part of the decision just comes from the gut.

Regarding the second question, I don't think I've ever reworked a story from one length to another, making a flash fiction piece into a short story, or a short story into a novel—or the reverse. It seems to me that stories find their length on their own, at least for me. It's one of the few things I don't have to worry about.

LC: You've had a number of academic books published over the years through major publishers like McGraw-Hill, Prentice Hall, and Ashgate Publishing, with topics ranging from literary theory to nineteenth-century French literature and culture. Have you moved away from academic writing to concentrate on fiction?

SDC: Yes, largely. That said, my creative writing seems to swirl around the same obsessions I pursued as an academic reader. The activities are complementary, although I've never learned more about literature than when I began to write it.

LC: Back in February 2013 you made mention of some projects you were working on: "more stories, some travel writing, and another novel." Do you intend to put out another story collection? Is the novel near completion and are you able to talk about it? Will it have the same well-honed edge of suspense that *Theory of Remainders* had?

SDC: Yes, yes, and yes. I have quite a number of irons in the fire. This fall I have a spate of short pieces coming out, including both stories and creative non-fiction (readers can follow my publications at www.sdcarpenter.com). The big project is, of course, the new novel. It's not "near completion" yet (I expect several more months at least of hard labor), but I'm very excited. It's set largely in the Midwest and deals with a young man wrestling with a traumatic event. And yes, it does employ suspense—which I find entirely compatible with compelling and literary fiction.

LC: Tell us about your latest non-fiction piece, which is published in this anthology.

SDC: "Danish as She is Spoke" erupted from my five-month teaching stint in Denmark, where I humiliated myself deeply on a daily basis. While it's a more humorous piece (I don't know why, but my travel pieces tend to humor), you'll find the same infatuation with language that informs *Theory of Remainders*. Whenever we think we have "mastered" language, lo and behold, it has mastered us.

DANISH AS SHE IS SPOKE

Scott Dominic Carpenter

As witches go, Fru Kjøller was better-looking than average—sandy blonde, late thirties, Viking cheekbones, a fetching black skirt. The clever disguise made it all the harder for us to hate her.

Her lips parted and the incantation began.

"*Reuhhdl greuhhdl meh fleuhhdl*," she murmured, rounding it off with a smile. "It's easy," she announced to the silent room. "Now repeat."

I shot a look at my neighbor—a plump woman with short hair and rabbit eyes. We'd taken the back row, but there were only six of us in the class, so it was hard to hide. Nobody wanted to respond, but the hag had tilted her head, and her smile was starting to thin at the edges, so we began our moos and groans, chanting like a chorus of stroke victims.

"Very good," she beamed, though we knew what was coming next. Whenever she failed to humiliate us as a group, she made us imitate that most famous of Danes—and soliloquize. "Now," she said, "one at a time."

By the time she got to me, I was ready. The trick was to pretend you'd just been shot and had to name your killer before the blood finished pulsing out of your chest.

"*Euhhh-kreuuuud-meuddd-fleuuuuuh*," I moaned.

Fru Kjøller eyed me as though watching a dog chase its own tail. "That's all right," she said, rocking back on her high heels, those handsome calves flexing. "Nobody really expects you to learn Danish anyway."

That was my introduction to the local tongue. In the course of an hour, we'd gone from simple greetings and survival phrases to less practical parlor tricks. *Rødgrød med fløde* meant "red gruel with double cream," a delicacy I never spotted on any restaurant menu. The phrase is a kind of tongue-twister, the gruel-and-cream test serving to impress foreigners with the unprounceability of the Danish language—and to provide Danes with mirth whenever you try. Maybe that's why Denmark ranks as the happiest of nations.

*

I'd come to Denmark for reasons I didn't fully understand, the first time for a meeting, then a couple days at a workshop, a seminar the following year… When an institute invited me to come and teach a class, I surprised myself by considering it.

"Why not?" I thought, though perhaps I should have asked a more useful question. Like: Why? Or: What would I actually *do* there? Of course, one could always visit the Little Mermaid. In Hans Christian Andersen's version of the tale, the fish-girl couldn't even speak—which meant that she and I had the same command of Danish.

"Come on," the director wheedled while I dithered. "It'll be *hyggelig*"—one of many words I'd never be able to pronounce.

Soon it was settled.

Not everyone has such a flexible job, my wife reminded me pointedly. She'd visit at the end of the semester.

"You're going away again?" my lawyer brother said. "Didn't you just have a vacation?"

"That was a sabbatical."

He gave a pinched smile. "Of course."

I arrived on the hottest day Copenhagen had seen in over three decades—the temperature spiking into the low nineties, most of the heat collecting in the fourth-floor walkup I was moving into. The front door of the building was propped open, and a paper sign had been taped to its glass: *Hold døren lukket*.

That, it occurred to me, was how to teach a language.

192

Instead of training us with inside jokes, the Danes should simply *label* their world, the way my mom used to sew tags into my clothing for summer camp. Heck, they already did it with streets and avenues, the metal signs embedded in the brick and stucco corners of the buildings. Why not everything else? I wanted Copenhagen with captions—each house marked as a *hus*, every train as a *tog*, stores as *buttiker*. Even cats and dogs could wear little nountags on their collars. After all, it's by matching words with the world that you understand language. There it was—*Hold døren lukket* posted on a *door held open*: what more could you ask for?

A bit of this labeled world existed at the supermarket, where eggs and pasta boldly proclaimed their identities, and where I liked to practice my language skills. On one of my first trips to the *Netto* shop, I got the attention of a dark-haired stock girl by pantomiming helplessness as I uttered the word "*Mælk*?" The truth is, I had a pretty fair idea of where the milk was kept. It was a fake question, designed to see if I could manufacture other questions later. My plan was to practice like mad before asking in what aisle they stocked red gruel with cream.

"Over there," she replied in English. "Behind the column."

That's the other problem if you want to learn Danish: the locals master English so early that even kids in elementary school make you feel like a dolt. In some countries it's sink or swim: if you don't pick up the language, you simply explode from never finding the bathroom. But in Denmark, people are always throwing you a lifeline. Or rather, a whole lifeboat. And then they climb over the gunnels to join you and make sure you're comfortable there. And to keep you off the oceanliner.

The students I was teaching—all Americans—surrendered early to the ubiquity of English. When I asked about their Danish, they looked down and coughed into their fists.

I complained to Helle, a colleague at the school where I taught. "Why do Danes always answer me in English?" I asked.

She leveled those icy baby blues on me. "When you speak Danish," she announced, "people feel embarrassed for you."

That put an end to speaking Danish with Helle.

By the way, I've changed all the names here so you don't sprain your tongue trying to say them.

So, I kept doing my homework, and after a couple of months I'd turned myself into a walking phrasebook—unfortunately, one modeled after *English as She is Spoke*, the nineteenth-century classic by a man who couldn't speak the language he taught, resulting in helpful dialogues like this:

How is that gentilman who you did speak by and by.

Is a German.

Tongh he is German, he speaks so much well italyan, french, spanish, and english, that among the Italyans, they believe him Italyan, he speak the frenche as the Frenches himselves. The Spanishesmen believe him Spanishing, and the Englishes, Englishman.

It is difficult to enjoy well so much several langages!

I, too, enjoyed so much my langage, and so I goed Danishing by and by.

One day when I came home from work, two kids wearing rubber boots charged out of the building. They were roughhousing and let the door swing closed behind them in blatant violation of the *Hold døren lukket* sign. I'd been finding the door closed a lot lately. A tall man with a leather satchel was retrieving mail from his box as I entered, so I made a show of propping the door open, giving him a little wink that meant, *Yep, those kids did it again.* Bobbing my head like the helpful immigrant I was, I showed how I'd remedied the problem. He grunted a string of complex syllables. "*Selv tak,*" I offered—

"you're welcome" being one of the few expressions I could manage. I was happy to be of service. He shook his head started up the stairwell.

Open doors are uncommon in Copenhagen. When I visited Danes, the doors to all the rooms were closed. Hallways looked like intimate insane asylums, presumably holding lunatic relatives or characters from Lars von Trier movies. Inside my own apartment, even when the doors gaped, they felt closed: traditional raised thresholds separated each room from the hallway, and they sent me into acrobatic tumbles in the middle of the night.

Figurative doors were equally tricky. It's easy to get into Denmark for a brief visit, but if you plan to stay a while, you might find parts of the culture locked and bolted. Immigration laws there are the most restrictive in Europe. Greg, an American who'd worked in Copenhagen for ten years, had just seen his request for permanent residency turned down—again. Although he'd married a Dane, fathered two Danish children, worked for three Danish companies, paid Danish taxes and, yes, even voted in Danish elections, he wasn't quite Danish enough. Not yet.

Did I mention that he also learned the language?

Picking up the local idiom is actually required, and anyone hankering for residency needs to pass a state language exam with an oral interview. So you *can* speak Danish with Danes—but only on the day they test you. After the exam, most Americans report that their colleagues keep addressing them in English.

Although no one wants you to practice it, Danish is oddly necessary. Sure, the tourist information is all in English—but good luck reading the application for the monthly train passes. Administrative paperwork—a local specialty—is typically not rendered in the language of Shakespeare. During my online banking sessions, I always worried I was wiring my salary to Nigeria. Danishing like the Danishesmen wasn't so easy.

On the other hand, people express surprise when you tell them you're trying to learn their tongue. *Why would you bother?* they ask (in English). *We're such a small country.*

It was a fair question. Why *did* I bother? I thought about that a lot while quizzing myself with flashcards or studying the shape of my tongue in the mirror. It was pointless. Almost. But I've always hated coming from a monoglot nation that expects everyone else in the world to sidle up and drawl things like, "Whoa, what's up, Jack?" It's healthy for Americans—especially middle-class white guys—to experience life as an outsider. It's important to meet other people on *their* terms, do things *their* way, in *their* language.

Isn't it?

When I told that to my wife over the phone, I could hear the roll of her eyes.

In any case, motives are moot, because Danes don't really want you to learn. They're proud of Danish's difficulty. It's a secret code, a shibboleth for figuring out who's part of the tribe. Sometimes I'd see colleagues chatting at the lunch table, and when I approached they'd exchange a glance and swerve into English. I recognized the pattern: it was how my parents used to shift gears when I walked into the room: Okay—now it's time for kid talk!

The crazy thing is that it shouldn't be so hard. In writing, Danish can be a lot like English. Remember *hold* for "hold"? Or *dør* for "door"? Sure, you have to get used to some perversities— saying "gruel the" instead of "the gruel," or figuring out how to avoid being rude when there's no word for "please." But with a decent dictionary (or the chicken's method of Google Translate) you can usually pick through it. The problem is pronunciation—the *red gruel with cream* thing. That's what makes you feel like you've just stumbled into a scene from *Beowulf* and you're taking language lessons from Grendel.

Pronouncing a new word for the first time was like going

on a blind date, filled with terror and humiliation. A word like *lagekagehuset* is pronounced "la-oh-kay-hoos-uh." The *lagekagehuset* ("layer-cake-house-the") was my local bakery, where the sales clerk sniggered every time I ordered a *snegl*—a word that should rhyme with "smile" but always came out sounding like an Orc's nickname from Middle Earth.

There was the time I went to buy open-faced sandwiches, known as *smørrebrød*. It was a tiny shop, and *smørrebrød* was the only thing they sold. The display case was overflowing with the stuff, and the signs on the wall cried out *Smørrebrød! Smørrebrød!*

"I'd like some *smørrebrød*, please," I said.

The woman behind the counter scrunched her nose. "What?"

Was it my fault Danish has more vowel sounds than there are herring in the North Sea? Even the Swedes and Norwegians complain about the way Danes pronounce things: at some point in Scandinavian history Danish pronunciation went out to pick up a pack of cigarettes and it never came back. It was abducted. Portraits of the old language should be placed on *mælk* cartons everywhere. Come back, come back! we'd cry. We'll *hold døren lukket* for you!

Nevertheless, I continued with my Danish lessons, working hard on the sounds. I didn't have the Viking witch anymore. I'd burned through two instructors, and now was in a "special" class with a jovial fellow named Mogens. He refused to crack down when I trotted out mutant pronunciations. "Very good," he'd say, like an uncle encouraging a toddler. It was only a problem if I strayed too far, if the words began to sound like gastric eruptions. Then an uncomfortable smile would spread across Mogen's face and he'd start examining his fingernails, buffing them on the front of his shirt.

I figured the problem was me. Then I met a long-term transplant from the US. He, too, still felt like an outsider because of the language. Jonathan had been in Denmark since the seventies, and he lived up in Elsinore, Hamlet's neighborhood. "After forty years," he said, "I guess it's no longer a love/hate relationship with Denmark. It's just sort of OK/not-so-bad." You'd never really be welcomed into the castle, he was saying, but you could get used to splashing around in the moat.

Jonathan was married to a Dane, and he introduced me to special family words like *mormor* ("mother's mother") and *farmor* ("father's mother"). Even these were tricky. *Mor*, a gentle, bosomy word, means "mother," but if you stretch out the pronunciation with a gulp, it turns to "murder"—the difference between maternity and matricide marked by the presence or absence of a death-rattly glottal stop.

I've cheated in that last example, because "murder" is written *m-o-r-d*. But the last letter is silent. Overall, d's are an enigma in Danish: some disappear, some are clipped, some go spongy, and some masquerade as other letters altogether. Most commonly you find it in a special soft variation. To produce it, imagine you're sitting in a dentist's chair with your tongue soaked with Novocain and your mouth full of clamps, and the hygienist has just asked you about your summer vacation. *That's* the sound.

The need to practice Danish changed my lifestyle. The fellow who cut my hair, a fourth-generation barber named Jesper, would chat a bit in the local idiom, so I found myself going in for regular groomings. As he snipped away the week's growth, I rolled out rehearsed sentences and strained to make out his replies. It was a bit like paying to have a friend. But it was cheaper than language teachers. And I felt good about how I looked.

In fact, I engaged in lots of purchases I wouldn't ordinarily make, just to practice. If you have that northern European look, there's an uncomfortable silence every time you enter a shop and they have to guess: Is he one of them or one of us?

Sometimes I could bluff for a word or two before blowing my cover, and sometimes salespeople would play along.

Toward the end of my semester, I stopped at a chocolate shop to pick up a hostess gift. The shopkeeper was a blonde woman, old enough to be the mother of my former teacher, Fru Kjøller. But she was gentler—more of a Glinda than a Wicked Witch. After my first syllables, she clasped her hands in indulgence and addressed me as though speaking to a Munchkin. Would I like to continue in English or Danish, she inquired. There was no one else in the shop, so I seized the opportunity, and we began the tortured process of choosing an assortment of morsels. On one tray sat rows of reddish blobs topped with a dot of white. The sight reminded me of something. "*Red gruel with cream*," I hazarded in Danish. She blinked at me, turned to the tray, then looked at me again. Suddenly her eyebrows rose and her teeth flashed. I had produced a joke, and she'd gotten it. For an instant, I kind of belonged.

I left the shop with chocolates in hand and a bounce in my step, stopping to check the store hours in case I wanted to return for another comedy routine. The sign announced: "Åben mandag—lørdag." Something nagged at me. The words for Monday and Saturday I knew. But *Åben*? I mulled that one over as I biked home. That A with the full moon overhead, it made an O sound, didn't it? And B's were often P's. A seismic tremor rumbled through my world.

Soon I found myself at the foot of my building, staring at the entrance. There were the old instructions, taped to the glass. Just then one of the neighbor kids came bursting out, letting the door swing closed, not even glancing at me to see if he'd get away with it.

That's when I realized my error. (Yes, any Danish reader has been scarlet with embarrassment for me since page one.) I'd misunderstood the *hold døren lukket* thing from the get-go. The door had been propped open that first day in the heat of

August, despite the posted order to keep it *closed*. I'd wanted the city labeled, but this door had been miscaptioned, like a poorly subtitled film.

And yet, it also somehow made sense, in a Danish sort of way. *Come in*, it beckoned with one hand, while with the other it brought you to a halt. It was just the thing to throw you off-balance, to make you stumble over the raised threshold. Both OK and not-so-bad.

It was like a door slightly ajar, one that Denmark was trying to close, but into which I had finally managed to stick my foot.

CONTRIBUTORS

Nicholas Litchfield is the founding editor of *Lowestoft Chronicle* and author of the novel *Swampjack Virus*. Born in Britain, he has worked in numerous countries as a librarian, journalist, and researcher. He lives in Western New York.

Peter Biello is the organizer of the Burlington Writers Workshop, Vermont's largest and most active public writing workshop. He's the managing editor of "The Best of the Burlington Writers Workshop." By day, he works as a producer/announcer at Vermont Public Radio, and work has appeared on PRI's This American Life, NPR's All Things Considered, Day to Day, Weekend Edition Sunday, and bustedhalo.com. He holds a BFA in Creative Writing from U-Maine Farmington and an MFA in Fiction from UNC-Wilmington.

Matt Nestor is a writer, editor and photographer living in New York. He is shopping around his first book, *Dropping In*, an undercover guide to twenty-five American colleges and universities.

David Hagerty has published a dozen short stories online and in print, including four in *Alfred Hitchcock's Mystery Magazine*. More of his work is available at www.davidhagerty.net. He is also polishing a political murder mystery that he expects will create a new sub-genre. Agents and editors are encouraged to query him.

During his academic career, **Dr. Sheldon Russell** authored twenty-five professional articles and co-authored the text, *An Interdisciplinary Approach to Reading and Mathematics*. He retired as Professor Emeritus from the University of Central Oklahoma in 2000. He has had nine novels published: *Empire*, a suspense novel; two historic frontier novels, *The Savage Trail* and *Requiem at Dawn*; *Dreams to Dust: A Tale of the Oklahoma Land Rush*; *The Dig: In Search of Coronado's Treasure*; and the Hook Runyon mystery series (*The Yard Dog*, *The Insane Train*, *Dead Man's Tunnel*, and *The Hanging of Samuel Ash*). Works in progress include: *The Woodcutter*, *Blood Rights*, and *Shrink Wrapped*.

He and his wife currently reside on the home ranch in northwestern Oklahoma where they both work daily at their respective crafts. Russell enjoys reading, gardening, and collecting his favorite books.

Victor Robert Lee has lived and traveled extensively in East Asia, South America and the former Soviet states—territories that serve as settings for his fiction. His current reporting from the Asia-Pacific region can be found in *The Diplomat* and elsewhere. He is the author of the literary espionage novel *Performance Anomalies*, described by *The Japan Times* as "a thoroughly original work of fiction."

After kicking around the West for a while (with stops in Spokane, Flagstaff, and Sedona), **Stephen Cloud** has settled in Albuquerque, where he's fixing up an old adobe, working on poems, and pondering the official New Mexico state question: "Red or green?" Recent publications include work in *Valparaiso Poetry Review*, *High Plains Journal*, *New Madrid*, *Lowestoft Chronicle*, and *Shenandoah*.

Soren A. Gauger is a Canadian who has lived for over a decade in Krakow, Poland. He has published two books of short fiction (*Hymns to Millionaires* via Twisted Spoon Press, and *Quatre Regards sur l'Enfant Jesus* with Ravenna Press) and translations of Polish writers (including Jerzy Ficowski, Bruno Jasienski and Wojciech Jagielski), as well as several dozen essays, stories, poems, and translations in journals in Europe and North America (including the *Chicago Review*, *Capilano Review*, *Contrary*, *Asymptote*, *Cossack*, *American Book Review*, and *Words Without Borders*). His first novel, *Neither/Nor*, will be published this October in Polish by Ha!Art Publishers.

Mona Zutshi Opubor is an Indian-American short story author and memoirist. Mona has work appearing in *Allusions of Innocence*, *Descant*, *The Kalahari Review*, and *Lowestoft Chronicle*. Mona received her B.A. in English Literature and her M.A. in Fiction Writing. She was a 2014 participant in the International Writing Program of The University of Iowa. Mona has lived with her husband and three children in Lagos, Nigeria, since 2011. She enjoys cooking spicy food, travel, doing charity work, and reading.

A former academic, **James Stark** lives with and writes about his characters in the often rainy, bleak environs of the Pacific Northwest of the US. Both he and his characters attempt to find resolution and redemption as they plod through life and the rain together. He has sent his characters out into the world by means of such publications as: *World City Stories*, *RiverLit*, *Straightjackets Magazine*, *221B Magazine*, *Pixelhose*, and *Lowestoft Chronicle*, among several others.

dl mattila, a resident of Virginia, holds the Master of Arts in Writing from Johns Hopkins University. Her poetry has been published in *Blast Furnace*, *Foothill: a journal of poetry*, *Lowestoft Chronicle*, and *Shot Glass Journal*, among others. Her work also appears on the Maier Museum of Art Ekphrastic Poetry webpage and at the Fisheries Museum of the Atlantic in Lunenburg, Nova Scotia.

After having made her career as a French professor at the University of Delaware, during which time she authored three academic books and co-edited four more, **Mary Donaldson-Evans** has decided to turn her attention from writing about fiction to writing fiction. Her non-academic pieces have been published by *The New York Times* (The Metropolitan Diary), AOL.com, and thestir.cafemom.com.

Robert Sachs is a writer living in Louisville, Kentucky. He earned an M.F.A. in Writing from Spalding University (2009). He serves on the board of Louisville Literary Arts and has been a board member of Sarabande Books, a not-for-profit book publisher. His short stories have appeared in *Mobius: The Journal of Social Change*, *Front Porch Review*, *Bound Off*, *The Writing Disorder*, *Red Fez*, *Blue Lake Review*, *Northern Liberties Review*, *Black Heart Magazine*, *Lowestoft Chronicle*, *Literary LEO*, and The 10th Annual WD Short Short Story Collection. His story "Blue Room With Woman," was an honorable mention finalist in the Glimmer Train November 2009 Short Story Award for New Writers. He was a semi-finalist in the Nineteenth Consecutive New Millennium Writing Competition.

David Havird is the author of two collections: *Map Home* (2013) and *Penelope's Design* (2010), which won the 2009 Robert Phillips Poetry Chapbook Prize. His poems have appeared in such periodicals as *Agni*, *The New Yorker*, *Poetry*, *Sewanee Review*, and *Yale Review*, and in anthologies: *The Southern Poetry Anthology, IV: Louisiana* and *Hard Lines: Rough South Poetry*. He teaches English at Centenary College of Louisiana. Since 2009 he has taught a course annually in Greece.

Originally from Ireland, **Kevin Quigley** has spent the past ten years traveling, working when he needs to, writing when he can. He is currently living in Iceland, where he hopes to do less of the former and more of the latter.

William Quincy Belle is just a guy. Nobody famous; nobody rich; just some guy who likes to periodically add his two cents worth with the hope, accounting for inflation, that $0.02 is not over-evaluating his contribution. He claims that at the heart of the writing process is some sort of (psychotic) urge to put it down on paper and likes to recite the following which so far he hasn't been able to attribute to anyone: "A writer is an egomaniac with low self-esteem." You will find Mr. Belle's unbridled stream of consciousness at http://wqebelle.blogspot.ca or https://twitter.com/wqbelle.

Robert Mangeot lives in Nashville with his wife and bevvy of animals. His fiction appears in various print and web outlets, including *Lowestoft Chronicle*, *Pure Slush*, and *Swamp Biscuits and Tea*, and *Mystery Writers of America presents ice cold: tales of intrigue from the Cold War*. His writing has won contests sponsored by the Chattanooga Writers' Guild, On The Premises, and Rocky Mountain Fiction Writers.

A graduate of the University of Maryland, **C.B. Heinemann**'s articles and stories have appeared in *The Washington Post*, *The Boston Globe*, *The Philadelphia Inquirer*, *Fate*, *One Million Stories*, *The Whistling Fire*, *The Battered Suitcase*, *Danse Macabre*, *Outside In Literary & Travel Magazine*, *Spilt Infinitive*, *Whistling Shade*, and *Lowestoft Chronicle*.

Jay Parini is a distinguished poet, novelist, biographer and critic. His books of poetry include *The Art of Subtraction: New and Selected Poems*, and he has written volumes of essays and critical studies, as well as biographies of John Steinbeck, Robert Frost, and William Faulkner. His novels include *Benjamin's Crossing*, *The Apprentice Lover*, *The Passages of H.M.*, and *The Last Station*, which was turned into an Academy Award-nominated film starring Helen Mirren, Christopher Plummer, and Paul Giamatti.

John Mueter is an educator, musician, composer and writer. His short fiction has been published by the *American Athenaeum*, *Freedom Forge Press*, the *Bibliotheca Alexandrina*, *Halfway Down the Stairs*, *Deep Water Literary Journal*, *Wilde Oats Journal*, and *Lowestoft Chronicle*. He currently teaches at the University of Kansas.

Robert Boucheron is an architect in Charlottesville, Virginia. His academic degrees are Harvard B.A. in English, and Yale M.Arch. His stories, essays and book reviews appear in *Atticus Review*, *The Bangalore Review*, *The Cossack Review*, *Digital Americana*, *Harvard Review*, *Lowestoft Chronicle*, *New Orleans Review*, *North Dakota Quarterly*, *Outside In Literary & Travel Magazine*, *Poydras Review* and other magazines. Website boucheronarch.com.

Allister Timms has an MFA from Stonecoast and lives with his wife and two daughters on the coast of Maine. He worked for many years as the copy editor for *Down East Magazine*. As a boy in Wales, he received elocution lessons but never encountered a talking parrot.

Michael C. Keith has authored more than twenty books on electronic media, among them *Talking Radio*, *Voices in the Purple Haze*, *Radio Cultures*, *Signals in the Air*, and the classic textbook *The Radio Station* (now *Keith's Radio Station*). He is also the author of an acclaimed memoir, *The Next Better Place*; a young adult novel, *Life is Falling Sideways*; and nine story collections. He has been nominated for the Pushcart Prize and PEN/O.Henry Award and is the recipient of numerous awards in his academic field. He teaches communication at Boston College. His website is www.michaelckeith.com.

A faculty member at the University of North Carolina School of the Arts, **Joe Mills** has published five volumes of poetry, most recently *This Miraculous Turning*.

Geoffrey B. Cain is an artist and educator who lives in Loleta, CA, where he writes novels, short stories, and poetry. His work has appeared in *Border Crossing*, the *Sonoma Mandala*, *Tom Cat*, *Deluge 6*, *Lowestoft Chronicle*, and other fine publications.

Raymond Abbott lives in Louisville, Kentucky. He publishes short stories and essays, even novels, whenever and wherever he can.

Scott Dominic Carpenter teaches French literature and critical theory at Carleton College in Northfield, MN. A Pushcart Prize nominee and a recipient of a Minnesota State Arts Board grant, his fiction has appeared in a broad array of literary journals. His books include the short story collection *This Jealous Earth* (MG Press) and the novel *Theory of Remainders* (Winter Goose Publishing), which was named to Kirkus Reviews' "Best Books of 2013." His website is located at www.sdcarpenter.com.

COPYRIGHT NOTES

"Break and Enter," copyright © 2014 by Peter Biello. First published in Lowestoft Chronicle, issue #17.

"Via Dolorosa," copyright © 2014 by Matt Nestor. First published in Lowestoft Chronicle, issue #18.

"Shutterbugs," copyright © 2014 by David Hagerty. First published in Lowestoft Chronicle, issue #19.

"A Conversation with Sheldon Russell," copyright © 2014 by Lowestoft Chronicle. First published in Lowestoft Chronicle, issue #18. Author photograph © Bob Bozarth.

"A Question Of The Tide," copyright © 2014 by Victor Robert Lee. First published in Lowestoft Chronicle, issue #19.

"Bangkok of the Mind," copyright © 2014 by Stephen Cloud. First published in Lowestoft Chronicle, issue #19.

"The Cambodian Void: An Apology," copyright © 2014 by Soren A. Gauger. First published in Lowestoft Chronicle, issue #19.

"My Driver, Sunday," copyright © 2014 by Mona Zutshi Opubor. First published in Lowestoft Chronicle, issue #19.

"Mobile Homeless," copyright © 2014 by James Stark. First published in Lowestoft Chronicle, issue #19.

"To The Passenger In Seat C," copyright © 2014 by dl mattila. First published in Lowestoft Chronicle, issue #17.

"Curious in Corsica: A Tale of Two Couples," copyright © 2014 by Mary Donaldson-Evans. First published in Lowestoft Chronicle, issue #20.

"Somewhere in the Heart of Rome," copyright © 2014 by Robert Sachs. First published in Lowestoft Chronicle, issue #17.

"Shooing Flies," copyright © 2014 by David Havird. First published in Lowestoft Chronicle, issue #20.

"A Farewell to Farms," copyright © 2014 by Kevin Quigley. First published in Lowestoft Chronicle, issue #18.

"Cathy Has Visitors," copyright © 2014 by William Quincy Belle. First published in Lowestoft Chronicle, issue #17.

"Uprisings at Cap d'Antibes," copyright © 2014 by Robert Mangeot. First published in Lowestoft Chronicle, issue #17.

"Rescue in the Mystical Mountains," copyright © 2014 by C.B. Heinemann. First published in Lowestoft Chronicle, issue #20.

"Midrash," copyright © 2013 by Jay Parini. First published in Lowestoft Chronicle, issue #14.

"A Conversation with Jay Parini," copyright © 2014 by Lowestoft Chronicle. First published in Lowestoft Chronicle, issue #18. Author photograph © Oliver Parini.

"The Sibyl," copyright © 2014 by John Mueter. First published in Lowestoft Chronicle, issue #18.

"Antique Roses," copyright © 2014 by Robert Boucheron. First published in Lowestoft Chronicle, issue #18.

"Survival of the Fittest," copyright © 2014 by Allister Timms. First published in Lowestoft Chronicle, issue #17.

"The Hill Behind the House," copyright © 2014 by Michael C. Keith. First published in Lowestoft Chronicle, issue #20.

"Enter the Travellers," copyright © 2014 by Joe Mills. First published in Lowestoft Chronicle, issue #20.

"Segway with the Bulls," copyright © 2014 by Geoffrey B. Cain. First published in Lowestoft Chronicle, issue #20.

"The High Colonic," copyright © 2014 by Raymond Abbott. First published in Lowestoft Chronicle, issue #20.

"A Conversation with Scott Dominic Carpenter," copyright © 2014 by Lowestoft Chronicle. First published in Lowestoft Chronicle, issue #20. Author photograph © Paul Carpenter.

"Danish as She is Spoke," copyright © 2014 by Scott Dominic Carpenter. First published in Lowestoft Chronicle, issue #20.

ACKNOWLEDGEMENTS

With special thanks to Amie McLaughlin for her priceless feedback and for all the proofreading she has done for the magazine over the last four years. Special thanks also to Tara for all her help and advice with the magazine and her outstanding design work, and to Jay Parini, Scott Dominic Carpenter, Sheldon Russell, James Reasoner, David Havird, and Michael C. Keith. The magazine wouldn't exist if it weren't for the marvelous contributors we've been fortunate to publish. Much gratitude to everyone who has contributed to the magazine.

Bon Voyage!

The first 'Best Of' from the acclaimed literary magazine!

Lowestoft Chronicle
2011 Anthology
Edited by Nicholas Litchfield

The world has gone digital. The physical book has been replaced by an electronic one; the family vacation has been replaced by the 'work retreat'. Today, the print anthology seems as unfashionable and outdated as the notion of travel for recreational purposes. In defiance of social trends and common sense we bring you the *LOWESTOFT CHRONICLE 2011 ANTHOLOGY*—a collection of our favorite stories, poems, and creative non-fiction pieces from the first year of our quarterly online magazine.

Lose yourself in the work of Lisa Abellera, Jennine Capó Crucet, Tim Conley, Michael Connor, Ron D'Alena, Brinna Deavellar, William Doreski, Laury A. Egan, Jack Frey, Katherine Hinkebein, Tyke Johnson, Michael C. Keith, Tom Mahony, Eric G. Müller, Jeremy Rich, Frank Roger, Phil Smith III, Davide Trame, Howard Waldman, and Aida Zilelian.

PRAISE FOR THE WORK IN
LOWESTOFT CHRONICLE 2011 ANTHOLOGY

"This is a fine anthology that I found both provocative and enjoyable. Highest praise: it made me want to write short stories again."
—Luke Rhinehart, author of the cult classic *The Dice Man*

"Michael Connor's 'Stevie and Louie' is a fun read about a young, single tourist in Austin… 'The Shooting Party' by Jack Frey is a story of a chance encounter in an exotic location that is both plausible and mysterious. It makes good use of dialogue and an inventive plot."
—*New York Journal of Books*

"Another good one is a tongue-in-cheek piece of fiction entitled 'The Last Election' by Frank Roger, about a group of men electing a pope as the planet around them is gradually being destroyed by earthquakes."
—*Newpages.com*

"Poems such as Laury Egan's 'Point No Point' show a journal that chooses poetry with keen regard to the specificity and the ache of place."
—Barth Landor, author of *A Week in Winter*

To order, visit www.lowestoftchronicle.com

Another 'Best Of' from the popular literary magazine!

Far-flung and Foreign

Edited by Nicholas Litchfield

Action, intrigue, romance and adventure—your boss may not be familiar with these words, and if he is he may not think they occur outside the workplace. This is your chance to tell him he's wrong. Beyond his wilting glare beckons the shimmering, fun-packed *FAR-FLUNG AND FOREIGN*.

Laden with dragons, lepers and Barbie dolls, and transporting readers to far-flung places, we proudly present the work of Vanessa Blakeslee, Will Buckingham, Joan L. Cannon, Lorraine Caputo, Martina Clark, Rijn Collins, Laury A. Egan, Michael Frissore, Bruce Gatenby, Kathie Giorgio, Charles Haddox, Rick Hartwell, Paul Kavanagh, Michael C. Keith, Benjamin Kensey, Wayne Lee, A. L. Means, Nicholas Rombes, Gordon West, and Scott Younkin. Also includes an exclusive interview with comic book writer Augustine Funnell.

PRAISE FOR THE WORK IN
FAR-FLUNG AND FOREIGN

"Hot off the press, and fresh from the mail, is this terrific anthology culled from *Lowestoft Chronicle* from 2011. The writing here is fresh, surprising, and alive. Not to be missed is the bittersweet interview with the author Augustine Funnell. (Please write more!) The book looks and feels great."
— Nicholas Rombes, acclaimed author of
A Cultural Dictionary of Punk: 1974-1982

"I immensely enjoyed 'The Adventures of Root Beer Float Man' by Michael Frissore. For poetry, try Wayne Lee's 'Ordinary Deckhand.'"
— *Newpages.com*

'I've enjoyed reading the *Chronicle*. 'I Like Your Deer's Moustache, and other Lithuanian Tales'...[is] a distinctly Baltic twist on mistaken identity. One of our most popular pieces."
— *My Audio Universe*
(Rijn Collin's story aired on the independent radio station KVMR).

To order, visit www.lowestoftchronicle.com

The third 'Best Of' in the acclaimed anthology series!

Intrepid Travelers

Edited by Nicholas Litchfield

Contributors include: Jada Ach, Jack Austin, Randal S. Brandt, Brian Conlon, Steve Gronert Ellerhoff, Bruce Gatenby, Sharleen Jonsson, Michael C. Keith, David Klein, Hector S. Koburn, Barth Landor, Robert Mangeot, dl mattila, Mark J. Mitchell, Lynn E. Palermo, James Reasoner, Tamara Kaye Sellman, Denise Thompson-Slaughter, and Dennis Vanvick, and Franz Wisner.

PRAISE FOR THE WORK IN INTREPID TRAVELERS

"Without a single stinker or filler piece in the bunch. I was extremely impressed with the variety and quality of the writing. *Intrepid Travelers* is a solid collection of funny and fine travel-themed stories, poetry, essays and interviews that easily fits in a back pocket or carry-on bag."
— *Examiner.com*

"Many short stories and poems here offer deeper meanings and address heavier topics. 'Something Like Culture Shock' by Dennis Vanvick…[has] good character development and a compelling story. 'Political Awakening, 1970' by Denise Thompson-Slaughter…it was refreshing to read a piece with this much depth. 'Pájaro Diablo' by Michael C. Keith…by the end, the reader is riveted to see what will happen next. Also features an interview with Randal S. Brandt…[which] has enough information and material to make for an entertaining read. Overall, this is full of great talent and exceptionally written pieces." — *The Review Review*

"Refreshing and well-written, *Intrepid Travelers* takes the reader to a wide variety of literary destinations, and makes even a confirmed hermit like me want to get up and go somewhere. Highly recommended."
— James Reasoner, *Rough Edges*

"Prepare for an adrenalin surge as a thief tries to escape from armed Mafia agents in Hector S. Koburn's fatalistic 'Bloody Driving Gloves,' Steve Gronert Ellerhoff's brilliantly quirky short story, 'Apophallation,' [and] Michael C. Keith's unexpectedly moving 'Pájaro Diablo.' *Intrepid Travelers* is a coruscating cornucopia of humour, drama and big, beautiful adventures. Highly original and entertaining."
—*Lancashire Evening Post*

"Contains a fascinating interview with Randal S. Brandt about his discovery of a lost manuscript by the author David Dodge. Excellent fiction, poetry, and non-fiction." — Nicholas Rombes, author of *Ramones* and *New Punk Cinema*

To order, visit www.lowestoftchronicle.com

Another 'Best Of' from Lowestoft's acclaimed literary magazine!

Somewhere, Sometime...

Edited by Nicholas Litchfield

Inside SOMEWHERE SOMETIME: A young exchange student and five fat ladies with a monkey brawl with a stalker after a tense train journey through eastern France. In Italy, love blossoms between an American tourist and a fifty-year-old man living in a cave on the island of Capri. A new eight-lane freeway brings a community to a sudden grinding halt…this anthology is crammed with scintillating tales!

Featuring the very best prose and poetry from the quarterly magazine *Lowestoft Chronicle*, and taking the reader to faraway and exotic places, we proudly present the work of Jason Braun, Nancy Caronia, Tim Conley, Brian Dennehy, Kim Farleigh, Sue Granzella, Ed Hamilton, Andrew House, Nick LaRocca, Rob McClure Smith, George Moore, Susan Moorhead, Jay Parini, Yvonne Pesquera, Thomas Piekarski, Chuck Redman, Michael Solomon, Jackie Strawbridge, and Laine Strutton. Includes exclusive interviews with acclaimed authors Michael C. Keith, Matthew P. Mayo, and James Reasoner.

PRAISE FOR THE WORK IN
SOMEWHERE, SOMETIME...

"The latest collection of prose and poetry from the *Lowestoft Chronicle* is a genuine pleasure. Take it with you on your next trip, no matter how far or flung. Nicholas Litchfield has put together something very special, something to celebrate, enjoy, savor."
— Jay Parini, bestselling author of
The Last Station and *Why Poetry Matters*

"Something to check out when you just want to read. For fans of short stories, creative non-fiction and poetry."
— *Radio FM4*

"What a lovely book. Well designed, thoughtfully laid out, and with a grand assortment of content."
— Matthew P. Mayo, Spur Award-winning author of
Tucker's Reckoning

To order, visit www.lowestoftchronicle.com

www.ingramcontent.com/pod-product-compliance
Lightning Source LLC
Chambersburg PA
CBHW031408250626
47155CB00004B/1461